Writing That Breaks Stones

Writing That Breaks Stones

AFRICAN CHILD SOLDIER NARRATIVES

Joya Uraizee

Michigan State University Press | *East Lansing*

MICHIGAN STATE UNIVERSITY PRESS
East Lansing, Michigan 48823-5245

LIBRARY OF CONGRESS CATALOGING-IN-PUBLICATION DATA
Names: Uraizee, Joya F. (Joya Farooq), 1961– author.
Title: Writing that breaks stones : African child soldier narratives / Joya Uraizee.
Description: East Lansing : Michigan State University Press, 2020.
| Includes bibliographical references.
Identifiers: LCCN 2019049199 | ISBN 978-1-61186-375-8 (paperback)
| ISBN 978-1-60917-649-5 (PDF) | ISBN 978-1-62895-410-4 (ePub)
| ISBN 978-1-62896-411-0 (Kindle)
Subjects: LCSH: Child soldiers—Africa—Personal narratives—History and criticism.
| Child soldiers in literature. | Ambiguity in literature.
| African literature—21st century—History and criticism.
Classification: LCC PL8010.6 .U73 2020 | DDC 809/.933581—dc23
LC record available at https://lccn.loc.gov/2019049199

Book design by Charlie Sharp, Sharp Des!gns, East Lansing, MI
Cover design by Shaun Allshouse, www.shaunallshouse.com

Visit Michigan State University Press at *www.msupress.org*

To children everywhere
forced into combat,
may you never fight again.

Contents

Preface

"When you're writing stories, you keep working with these horrible, archaic and hyperbolic things. It's when you stop writing the story and realize these things happen in real life, that's when it's tough. You've got to distance yourself" (Leiren-Young). This realization made it difficult for Vietnamese-Canadian director Kim Nguyen to write and direct *War Witch* / *Rebelle* (2012), a movie about a child soldier in the Democratic Republic of the Congo. Inspired by the lives of Luther and Johnny Htoo, twin brothers from Burma/Myanmar forced to fight in a guerrilla unit against the Burmese army, the movie was selected as Canada's entry for the Oscars' Best Foreign Language Film that year. It tells the story of Komona, a young Congolese girl kidnapped and forced to fight with a group of rebel soldiers, and her search for peace and freedom. Despite scenes containing graphic violence, Komona's story includes magical elements, such as ghosts that appear and disappear, and lovers haunted by demons of the past.

Narratives about children like Komona, whose life experiences include encounters with unspeakable horror, are the subject of

this book. For the past fifteen years, I have been concerned with
the way young adults in Africa write about childhood experiences
that were horrifying. Both during my numerous meetings with
former child soldiers in Sierra Leone and elsewhere, and in the
course of my scholarly investigations of the topic, I was guided, in
part, by former child soldier and memoir writer China Keitetsi's
insights about her writing process. Long after she stopped being a
child soldier with Uganda's National Resistance Army (as it existed
then) she found it hard to process her experiences because, as she
pointed out in her interview with me:

> You cannot talk about everything that has happened to you; you
> go to your grave with it. There is a lot of shame, even for hun-
> dreds of years. You don't know how the world will look at you.
> However, for me, to write and talk about my experiences was the
> best medicine. . . . Once you talk about the painful things, then
> the pain lessens and you learn to live with it.

While I believe that Keitetsi makes a good case for the "medici-
nal" benefits of life writing by former African child soldiers, I am
struck by the fact that the forms their narratives take are varied and
diverse. I have, during my research process, become convinced
that memoirs produced by young adults who were once soldiers,
as well as fiction written by novelists in Africa about child soldiers,
center on narrative uncertainty. Despite their preference for lin-
earity and chronological consistency, their narratives are often
shot through with ambivalences and contradictions that make the
reading experience unsettling. This ambivalence marks both life
writing by former African child soldiers and novels about fictional
child soldiers. Circular narratives, repetitive imagery, interior
monologues, and unexplained confrontations dominate African
child soldier fiction, often leaving questions of culpability and

morality murky and unclear. Memoirs and novels about African child soldiers share this focus on narrative uncertainty.

In this book, I compare fiction and nonfiction about African children at war by framing them within the motifs of ambivalence and uncertainty. Memoirs and novels, when studied together, reveal nuanced and diverse perspectives on both the suffering of the children themselves and their abilities to resist dehumanization and to define themselves on their own terms (Coundouriotis, *People's Right* 2). The narratives resist easy categorization, the speaking voices within them being at once confident and uncertain, self-aware and self-deluded, idealistic and cynical. Nestled within the African war novel genre, these narratives circulate globally, contributing, as they do so, to a larger discourse on human rights and social justice. Both a subgenre within the African war novel and part of a global phenomenon, the African child soldier narrative presents its young protagonists as both victims and perpetrators, both culpable for murder and innocent of crime. The narratives are didactic, cynical, naturalistic, and surrealistic; they contain binary oppositions, dystopic imagery, ethical quandaries, and emotional appeals to their readers. War, in these narratives, is absurd and meaningless, while the children themselves frequently retain strong cultural connections to their communities.

The absurdities of war notwithstanding, combat experiences were terrifying and traumatizing for the children. PTSD-induced "dissociative amnesia" (Bremner 220) made remembering precise details about their experiences difficult, yet often they were able to recollect, in vivid detail, the events themselves. This was partly because writing about traumatic past experiences was, as I indicated earlier, therapeutic. In her interview with me, China Keltetsi described the weight of her past memories as a child soldier as if they were stones weighing down heavily on her shoulders. She described her writing process as therapeutic, a situation that marks it, I would argue, as a specific kind of "memory work." As Ananya Kabir suggests, within South Asian narratives about the trauma of the partition of India, songs and dances harkening back to a pretraumatic past frequently "erupted," and eventually such eruptions became "intrinsic to South Asian memory work in the face of trauma" (65). Likewise, within African narratives about children's experiences of war, brief, unexplained references to other events "erupt" within the narratives, in ways that are ambiguous and unsettling to the reader. This ambiguity or uncertainty is the distinguishing characteristic of the African child soldier narrative.

In the chapters that follow, I explore at length twelve child soldier narratives that deal with trauma and uncertainty. I examine six memoirs that describe children's experiences of war and that use contradictory images and direct addresses to the readers in order to do so. Three of those memoirs, namely, Ugandan-Danish China Keitetsi's *Child Soldier,* Eritrean-German Senait Mehari's *Heart of Fire,* and Sierra Leonean–American Ishmael Beah's *A Long Way Gone,* are narratives of "false" combat. This is because they contain narrative contradictions pertaining to both the experience of combat and the cultural contexts in which that combat unfolds. In them, the African child soldier appears as both victim and perpetrator, and the combat itself becomes somewhat ambiguous. The other three memoirs I analyze in this book are collaborative in nature and use the protagonist's combat experience as the "backdrop" for a larger ideological issue. They were written by former child soldiers, with assistance from European or North American cowriters. South Sudanese Emmanuel Jal wrote *War Child* with British journalist Meghan Lloyd Davies; Ugandan Grace Akallo wrote *Girl Soldier* with American evangelist Faith McDonnell; and Mariatu Kamara, a young Sierra Leonean girl attacked by rebel soldiers, wrote *A Bite of the Mango* assisted by Canadian journalist Susan McClelland. All three collaborative memoirs provide graphic descriptions of conflict, but eventually that experience becomes the means to explore such survival strategies as making music about war (in *War Child*), transforming oneself through faith (in *Girl Soldier*), or creating a supportive community (in *A Bite of the Mango*). Whether individually written or collaborative, all six memoirs connect the personal narratives of the children to larger, more public issues.

The six novels that I also analyze in this book have child soldier protagonists with ambiguous loyalties and whose conflicts unfold within dystopic landscapes. Three of those six novels, namely, *Allah Is Not Obliged* (by Ivoirian Ahmadou Kourouma), *Johnny Mad Dog* (by Congolese-American Emmanuel Dongala), and *Beasts of No Nation* (by American Uzodinma Iweala) are "uncertain" narratives. Despite the graphic and realistic descriptions of the violence contained within their pages, the character of Johnny, the protagonist of *Johnny Mad Dog,* contains contradictions that aren't fully resolved. Kourouma's protagonist, Birahima, makes frequent references to historical events and rebel leaders, and Iweala's protagonist, Agu, provides copious details of his life during and before the war. However, their voices are cynical and unreliable, and their narratives frequently allude to this. Three other novels, namely, *Moses, Citizen, and Me* (by Sierra Leonean–British Delia Jarrett-Macauley), *Half of a Yellow Sun* (by Nigerian Chimamanda Adichie), and *Song for Night* (by Nigerian-British Chris Abani), are "dystopic" novels. They represent the child in combat in nightmarish ways. Citizen, the child soldier in *Moses, Citizen, and Me,* is too traumatized to talk, and protagonist Julia can only connect to him by putting him, narratively speaking, inside her head. While much of the narrative of *Half of a Yellow Sun* is focused on how civilians coped during the Nigerian-Biafran war, Ugwu's brief combat experience leaves him with nightmares about the rape and mutilation of women's bodies. The dead child soldier My Luck, the protagonist of *Song for Night*, who tells his story while inhabiting a sort of life-in-death limbo, frequently calls attention to his own unreliability. The protagonists of all six novels have ambiguous loyalties, and the narratives about them are fragmented and absurd. By comparing these six novels to the six memoirs mentioned earlier, I call attention to the complexities within the child soldier narrative, a subgenre within the African war narrative that is marked by fragmentation and ambiguity.

Acknowledgments

This book could not have been written without the constant support of colleagues, family, and friends. First, I owe a debt of gratitude to the following professors at Makerere University, Kampala, Uganda: Professors Aaron Mushengyezi (Dean, School of Literature, Languages and Communication), Susan Kiguli (Head, Department of Literature), Ernest Okello Ogwang (former Vice Chancellor), Dominica Dipio (Department of Literature), as well as Mahmood Mamdani, Executive Director of the Makerere Institute of Social Research in Kampala. I also appreciate all the support I got from my friends in the greater Ugandan community, Mr. Mohiuddin Razvi, Mr. Dawood Razvi, and Yusuf. Likewise, I deeply appreciate the insights of the following faculty members at Fourah Bay College, University of Sierra Leone, in Freetown, Sierra Leone: Professors Kenneth Osho (Department of English), Elizabeth Kamara (Department of English), J. D. Allie (Department of History), Sylvanus Spencer (Head, Department of History), and Alfred Jarrett (Head, Department of Sociology and Social Work). I received lots of help, too, from the greater Sierra Leonean community, including Professor Arthur Hollist (of the University of Tampa, Tampa, Florida),

Professor Ernest Cole (of Hope College, Holland, Michigan), Ms. Linsey Warburton (United Kingdom), Mr. Peter Andersen (former Counsel for the Special Court for Sierra Leone), Mr. Brima Sheriff (former Commissioner of Amnesty International, Sierra Leone), Mr. Gbanabom Hallowell (Director of the Sierra Leone Broadcasting Association), Mr. Juma Abu (former Director of Children Associated with War, Sierra Leone), Mr. Edward Jusu (National Director, Health for All Coalition, Sierra Leone), Mr. Mohamed Jalloh (former UNICEF officer in Sierra Leone), Mr. Dehunge Shiaka (Director of the Ministry of Social Welfare, Gender and Children's Affairs in Freetown), and Ms. Valnora Edwin (at the Campaign for Good Governance, Freetown, Sierra Leone). I also gained valuable insights from Mr. Kabba Williams (former child soldier in Sierra Leone), Mr. Bashiru Conteh (former child soldier in Sierra Leone), Dr. Sandra Lako (physician at Ola During Children's Hospital, Freetown, Sierra Leone), Mrs. Gladys England (owner of the Oasis Juice Bar in Freetown, Sierra Leone), and Mr. Osman Bah. Earlier on in my project, I benefited greatly from discussions with Professors Neville Smith, Kevin Goddard, Sheena Goddard, Sisi Magaqi, and Mary West, my colleagues at Nelson Mandela Metropolitan University in Port Elizabeth, South Africa, with whom I was fortunate to spend six months during my 2008 Fulbright Fellowship there.

Thanks are due to Professors Kenneth Harrow, Lokangaka Losambe, Juliana Nfah-Abbenyi, Moradewun Adejunmobi, Ketu Katrak, and Kanika Batra, my friends and colleagues at the African Literature Association, who have given me much-needed advice and suggestions. I am deeply indebted also to my colleagues at Saint Louis University, particularly, Professors Toby Benis and Jonathan Sawday in the Department of English, Professor Michael Barber in the Department of Philosophy, Professor Christopher Duncan in the Department of Political Science, Professor Penny

Weiss in the Department of Women and Gender Studies, and Professor George Ndege in the Department of History. I also wish to thank my former colleagues in the Department of English, Professors Sara van den Berg and Joseph Weixlmann, and my late colleagues Professor Georgia Johnston in the Department of English and Professor Michal Rozbicki in the Center for Intercultural Studies. I am very thankful to all of them for their help, encouragement, and financial support.

Thanks are also due to the National Center for Faculty Diversity and Development for its encouragement and support as I neared the end of the writing process. In particular, I owe a debt of gratitude to Prof. Marta Robertson, my coach in its summer 2019 Faculty Success Program, as well as Dr. Jim Ji, Dr. Ravit Reichman, and Dr. Kevin Deegan-Krause, my colleagues in that program.

Finally, thanks are due to my husband Farooq, my daughter Aisha, my son Omar, and my extended family and friends in St. Louis and elsewhere, for their unwavering support.

The author is grateful to the following publishers for permission to reprint material that they published originally, or for which they hold copyright.

- The excerpts from *Allah Is Not Obliged* by Ahmadou Kourouma, translated by Frank Wynne, translation copyright © 2006 by Frank Wynne, are used by permission of Anchor Books, an imprint of the Knopf Doubleday Publishing Group, a division of Penguin Random House LLC. All rights reserved.
- The excerpts from *Beasts of No Nation* by Uzodinma Iweala, copyright © 2005 by Uzodinma Iweala, are reprinted by permission of HarperCollins Publishers.
- The quotations from *The Bite of the Mango* ©2008 by

Mariatu Kamara with Susan McClelland (text); first
published by Annick Press, Ltd; all rights reserved; are used
by permission (for USA, Philippines, Canada, Australia, and
New Zealand).

- The quotations from © Mariatu Kamara with Susan
  McClelland, 2008, *The Bite of the Mango,* Bloomsbury
  Publishing Plc, are used by permission (for the world
  excluding USA, Philippines, Canada, Australia, and New
  Zealand).
- The quotations from *Child Soldier: Fighting for My Life* ©
  2004 by China Keitetsi, published by Souvenir Press, are
  used by permission.
- The quotations from *Girl Soldier: A Story of Hope for
  Northern Uganda's Children* © 2007 by Faith J. H. McDonnell
  and Grace Akallo, Baker Publishing Group, are used by
  permission.
- The quotations from *Half of a Yellow Sun* by Chimamanda
  Ngozi Adichie, copyright © 2006 by Chimamanda Ngozi
  Adichie, are used by permission of Alfred A. Knopf, an
  imprint of the Knopf Doubleday Publishing Group, a
  division of Penguin Random House LLC. All rights reserved
  (for USA, Canada, and the Philippines).
- The quotations from *Half of a Yellow Sun* by Chimamanda
  Ngozi Adichie are reprinted by permission of HarperCollins
  Publishers Ltd. © Chimamanda Ngozi Adichie, 2006 (for
  the world excluding USA, Canada, and Philippines).
- The quotations from *Heart of Fire* © 2006 by Senait Mehari,
  translated by Christine Lo; first published in English by
  Profile Books Ltd., are used by permission.
- Reprinted by permission of Farrar, Straus and Giroux:
  excerpts from *Johnny Mad Dog* by Emmanuel Dongala,

reprinted by permission of Vintage Canada / Random House Canada, a division of Penguin Random House Canada Limited. All rights reserved.

- The quotations from *They Poured Fire on Us from the Sky* by Benjamin Ajak, Alephonsion Deng, Benson Deng, Judy A. Bernstein, copyright © 2005, 2006, 2015, are reprinted by permission of PublicAffairs, an imprint of Perseus Books, LLC, a subsidiary of Hachette Book Group, Inc.
- The quotations from *War Child: A Child Soldier's Story* © 2009 by Emmanuel Jal are reprinted by permission of St. Martin's Griffin, an imprint of St. Martin's Press. All Rights Reserved.

CHAPTER 1

War Narratives and African Children

Anyone who has ever looked into the glazed eyes of a soldier
dying on the battlefield will think hard before starting a war.

—Otto von Bismarck

n 1925, a young teacher in Lesotho named Thomas Mokopu
Mofolo published a novel entitled *Chaka,* written in his native
Sesotho. *Chaka,* which was Mofolo's third novel in Sesotho
and was sixteen years in the making, is a fictionalized historical
biography of the great nineteenth-century Zulu chief Shaka,
who slowly transforms himself from young novice to proud and
ruthless commander, battling an unjust world. In 1931 *Chaka* was
translated into English and French (Coundouriotis, *People's Right*
26). Now regarded by scholars as a classic, Mofolo's *Chaka* is a
blend of oral and written historical traditions and is sometimes
taken to be the first modern African war novel (Coundouriotis,
"Arrested Historicization" 197). Eleni Coundouriotis has defined
the African war novel as a genre that, unlike the African bildungsroman, captures "the people's perspective" and provides a "collective account of ordinary people in the historical transitions

from colonialism to independence and the post-independence and globalizing eras. It focuses on the politically marginalized, trying to imagine a perspective from below" (*People's Right* 1–2). Coundouriotis also suggests that this genre "addresses a national audience, takes most often the rural poor as its subject, and, although it records violence that shakes the nation to its core, also recommits to the nation with less skepticism" (17). If *Chaka* is an early example of the African war novel, then it is so because, as Coundouriotis points out, its protagonist, Chaka, isn't just a larger-than-life savior of the Zulu people against the ravages of tyrannical rulers. He is also a bloodthirsty leader who kills thousands of his own people in cruel ways (Coundouriotis, "Arrested Historicization" 198), and his dehumanization unfolds within a colonial historical context during which extreme acts of violence were commonplace. While the young Chaka is presented as a likable underdog who is terribly mistreated, the mature Chaka appears to be a ruthless and monomaniacal dictator who thinks nothing of murdering his own mother in order to become supreme ruler. Chaka's ascent to, and descent from, supreme power in Africa, amid a constantly reshaping landscape, has sometimes been read as a "rerouting" of postcolonial African history via an "ecological archive of southern Africa" (Sides 441). Critics have commented on Mofolo's ability to provide detailed descriptions of the horrific and exciting situations his protagonist faced, as well as the corrupting influence of evil in his life (Malaba 61–62). Others have praised the novel's cultural specificity (its depiction of Chaka's political acumen and vision of Zulu nationhood) (Vassilatos 163), and its "transculturation" (the way it lent itself to constant rewritings and recreations by later writers, like Léopold Sédar Senghor) (161). Above all, Mofolo's focus on both the salutary and the unsavory aspects of Chaka's character set the stage for what Coundouriotis describes as one of the hallmarks of the African war novel, namely, its ability to capture, rhetorically, "a sense of democratic possibility when the conditions of war can be overcome" by engaging with the poor (*People's Right* 5). *Chaka* was written between 1909 and 1910, and soon after it was completed, Mofolo submitted it to the Paris Evangelical Missionary Society of Lesotho, which refused to publish it for fifteen years. As a result, it wasn't published till 1925 (Sides 444). In 1940, it was translated into French by Victor Ellenberger. The French translation popularized the story, and it became well known throughout Francophone Africa. Léopold Sédar Senghor wrote a poem entitled "Chaka" in 1956, and Mazizi Kunene wrote an epic entitled *Emperor Shaka the Great* in 1979 (Malaba 62–64). In 1981, it was translated into English by D. P. Kunene. Unfortunately, however, Mofolo was unable to make a living as a writer; he died in 1948 without achieving any fame. It would take several decades before anything resembling a "sense of democratic possibility" would ensue in southern Africa.

From the 1960s through the 1990s, numerous other African war novels followed *Chaka*.[1] In many of them the focus is as much on the suffering caused by war as on the transformation of the protagonist. This attention to human suffering is partly because the African war novel envisions, as Coundouriotis suggests, the creation of a "just society" (Coundouriotis, *People's Right* 10–12). In 1985, four years after *Chaka* was translated into English, Nigerian novelist and activist Ken Saro-Wiwa published, via his own publishing house, Saros International, a satirical account of the Nigerian civil war from the point of view of Mene, an uneducated, teenage boy. That novel, later to become famous as *Sozaboy: A Novel in Rotten English,* is noteworthy not just because of its subject matter but also because of its language. The novel's vocabulary and syntax were entirely invented by Saro-Wiwa, and brought the novel both praise and criticism. Charles Nnolim labeled the language "unconventional," Asomwan Adagboyin found it to be quite authentic, while Jago Morrison suggested that it was a symptom of Mene's ignorance (21–22). This critical focus on the novel's language, however, deflects attention away from its other unique features. Instead of the hypermasculine Chaka, who learns to kill without reservations, we have the hesitant and confused Mene, who never really understands why he is fighting and who survives but loses everything. Despite the fact that Mene's age in the novel is somewhat indeterminate, *Sozaboy* is often taken to be the precursor of the contemporary African child soldier narrative (Coundouriotis, "Arrested Historicization" 195).

The contemporary African child soldier narrative is the focus of this book. I contend that novels and memoirs that depict African children either actively fighting in wars, or being adversely affected by conflicts, break and build bridges in the global public sphere. By this I mean that they simultaneously connect and disconnect with their readers in unique ways. The memoirs do so by using narrative contradictions, namely, binary oppositions, repeated images and phrases, and direct addresses to their readers. The novels do so via narrative uncertainty, such as ambiguous characterization, circular plots, and dystopic imagery. Both the memoirs and the novels make appeals to their local and global communities on several levels at once—the aesthetic, the ethical, and the emotional. Finally, they have strong cultural connections to their local public spheres and describe individual stories of abuse while also evoking larger histories.

Ambiguity and dystopic imagery abound in *Sozaboy.* The novel begins with Mene deciding to fight in the Biafran war, because he thinks his soldier's uniform will win him fame and glory. He spends years fighting in wretched conditions (often without adequate food, water, or weapons), and eventually most of his friends die. He never really understands the Biafran cause and eventually decides to return to his hometown to look for his newlywed wife and aging mother. By then his community has been told that he has died in an explosion; therefore, when he returns, his former friends and neighbors take him for a ghost and shun him. Right at the end of the narrative he despairs when he learns that soon after the war started, his family was killed in a bomb blast.

Mene's transformation, from swashbuckling teenager to revenant (Morrison 23), reveals a narrative situation that Eleni Coundouriotis has labeled "arrested historicization." By this she means a fictional situation in which the protagonist never completely understands all the forces and situations arrayed against him or her ("Arrested Historicization" 199). This lack of understanding on the part of the protagonist is the distinguishing feature of the African child soldier narrative, and it manifests itself via formal and stylistic ambiguities. Not only is the child soldier's degree of innocence or victimization ambiguous, but the uncertainty surrounding his culpability manifests itself in the narrative via stylistic contradictions, repetition, narrative uncertainty, and dystopic imagery, among other things.

African Child Soldier Narratives

Both African child soldier novels and African child soldier memoirs show what many social scientists already know, that in communities in which national governments are weak and access to jobs and education is inadequate, children are susceptible to recruitment by militias (Kearney 71). Scholars agree that exact numbers of children fighting in wars is difficult to pin down; however, in 2016, scholars estimated that hundreds of thousands of boys and girls under the age of eighteen had been recruited, by sixty-one parties to conflict worldwide ("Questions and Answers").

In 2010, that number was approximately two hundred thousand (Gettleman 6). These "small soldiers" were used as combatants, messengers, porters, cooks, and sex slaves ("Questions and Answers").[2] While it is true that most of these children were forced, by unscrupulous adults, to join militias, in practice, many had few other options available to them. Often such children were desperately seeking food and shelter or opportunities to exact revenge against their parents' killers (Honwana 37). Force and terror were used to keep them in place (50), and, as Alcinda Honwana has shown, the conflicts created a "destructive, and problematic form of masculinity that was not aligned with civil society in peacetime" (53). Children were taught to dehumanize their enemies and obeyed their commanders out of a combination of fear and drug-induced forgetfulness (58).[3] Even when they escaped successfully, their violation of social norms led to frequent rejections by their extended families (110). Honwana points out that in Mozambique and Angola, adults and children who were associated with war were not accepted back into their societies because they were considered polluted (105). Likewise, a majority of the seventy-one thousand Sierra Leonean ex-combatants who were disarmed and demobilized in 2005 were unable to find jobs or live with their families. The vast majority became urban gangsters ("Sierra Leone Legacy"). Often, African children who were involved in violent incidents were viewed as troublesome and dangerous at best, and evil and demonic at worst (de Boeck and Honwana 10). Therefore, they were not rehabilitated and became, in essence, outlaws protected by their warlords until they were killed in combat.

Across the globe, modernist memoirs and novels have depicted the brutalization of children experiencing difficult social circumstances. Writing about the post–World War II global rise in struggles for self-determination and equality, Kay Schaffer and

Sidonie Smith argue that personal narratives written by ordinary people often inspired political and social movements for change (15). Summarizing the processes that led to the passing of significant international human rights laws (such as the Convention on the Rights of the Child, for example), Schaffer and Smith point out that "personal witnessing" actually led to the creation of several new international rights (16). This is because in remembering past atrocities, communities narrate "alternative or counter-histories" (17) that enable them to claim "new identities and assert their participation in the public sphere" (19). Within texts where the remembering of past trauma is represented fictionally, human rights issues can be represented, as Alexandra Moore and Elizabeth Goldberg argue, from "multiple, shifting cultural perspectives" (2). Indeed, literary texts and life writing about human rights violations can provide what Joseph Slaughter has called "the restorative powers of storytelling" (142). Describing the work of the Truth and Reconciliation Commission in South Africa in the 1990s, Slaughter argues that the personal narratives that resulted from the commission's work had "an inherent force of their own . . . a will to be told"; therefore, they became part of South Africa's national history (143). Although the commission produced an exceptional kind of storytelling, the public arena is, as Slaughter argues, a space that connects individual stories with national narratives (145). That space (what Slaughter calls the "liberal, national public sphere") is crucial to the formation and discussion of human rights and their violations because it straddles the boundaries between private and public arenas (148). The public sphere can be a site for both the veneration and the violation of human rights; therefore, narratives from around the world that deal with the nature of such rights and the political formations that they contain (nations and communities) are an integral part of that space.[4]

Narrative Uncertainty

Given their obvious connections to human rights issues, African child soldier narratives are often received, in the public sphere, as simplistic "victim narratives" where "responsibility for the committing of atrocity by the child soldier is largely disclaimed as either abuse the child has suffered, or the result of drug addiction from which the child must be rehabilitated" (Coundouriotis, "Arrested Historicization" 192). When examined more closely, however, African child soldier memoirs and novels present complex and contradictory notions of agency and culpability. In my second chapter, I argue that China Keitetsi's *Child Soldier,* Senait Mehari's *Heart of Fire,* and Ishmael Beah's *A Long Way Gone* represent a specific kind of child soldier memoir that I am calling the narrative of false combat. Despite the fact that all three were written by former African child soldiers, some readers regarded them as fabrications, written for the sole purpose of providing material benefits for their authors (such as immigration clearance to a European or North American country).[5] While some readers cast doubts on the veracity of the authors' combat experiences, others suggested that the cultural contexts in which the combat took place were inaccurately depicted. This focus on factual veracity is partly a result, I would argue, of the ways the narratives are written. All three memoirs present the child soldier as both victim and perpetrator, both culpable of murder and mayhem and innocent of such charges. Their narratives, therefore, use imagery and direct addresses in ambiguous ways.

By turns didactic and cynical, naturalistic and surrealistic, many African child soldier narratives make only oblique references to war and morality. As Mary Louise Pratt suggests, most readers of narratives about children experiencing violence understand that they are reading subjective accounts of abuses, and that other participants might have different versions of the same stories (41). What is perhaps less obvious, however, is the degree of narrative uncertainty that these texts reflect. In my third chapter, I analyze three memoirs written by former child soldiers with some help from European or North American cowriters. South Sudanese former child soldier Emmanuel Jal cowrote his memoir, *War Child*, with help from British journalist Meghan Lloyd Davies. Ugandan Grace Akallo, a former child soldier, cowrote a memoir named *Girl Soldier* with American evangelist Faith McDonnell. Mariatu Kamara, a young Sierra Leonean girl attacked by rebel soldiers, cowrote her memoir, *A Bite of the Mango*, with help from Canadian journalist Susan McClelland. All three collaborative memoirs provide graphic descriptions of conflict as a backdrop for something else. By this I mean that in the public sphere, each story about combat becomes less important than some other issue. Jal's memoir was written after he had already made a name for himself as a rapper, and his writing was influenced by his work within the music industry. *Girl Soldier* is the product of a rather unequal partnership. American missionary Faith McDonnell initiated and managed the collaboration; thus, the details of Akallo's combat experience become the means to emphasize the transformative nature of her faith. By contrast, Canadian journalist Susan McClelland painstakingly recorded the details of Kamara's interactions with rebel soldiers and her subsequent recovery, using the skills she had honed during her work with other women who had survived adversity. What emerges in *A Bite of the Mango*, therefore, is a slice of a life, particularly the survivor's will to survive. Both chapters 2 and 3 of this book reveal how African memoirs about child soldiers connect personal narratives to larger atrocities unfolding in the public arena.

African child soldier novels, like memoirs written by former African child soldiers, can be read didactically, as cautionary tales about the ways in which children who commit horrific crimes may or may not be rehabilitated in the public arena. As Slaughter has shown, the eighteenth-century European bildungsroman filled a democratic function, namely, "demarginaliz[ing] the historically marginalized individual" (157) by including him or her within the public sphere. However, the African child soldier novel, unlike its eighteenth-century European counterpart, uses narrative uncertainty in a way that frequently disorients its readers. The three novels I examine in chapter 4, *Allah Is Not Obliged* (by Ahmadou Kourouma), *Johnny Mad Dog* (by Emmanuel Dongala), and *Beasts of No Nation* (by Uzodinma Iweala), have ambiguous plots. The violence that surrounds Johnny and his gang is described in chilling, realistic detail, and these details are based on Dongala's personal experiences and observations when he was a chemistry professor in Brazzaville, Republic of Congo. Nevertheless, Johnny's character is shot through with ambiguities and contradictions that aren't fully resolved. Both Ivoirian novelist Ahmadou Kourouma and American-Nigerian Uzodinma Iweala had read about child soldiers fighting in West Africa and used those insights to develop their characterizations of Birahima (in *Allah Is Not Obliged*), and Agu (in *Beasts of No Nation*). Kourouma's protagonist, Birahima, weaves pure historical commentary into his narrative, naming real West African rebel leaders like Charles Taylor and Samuel Doe, and actual war tactics like the use of fetishes, all of which give a realistic feel to his narrative. When Iweala was an undergraduate student, he won a fellowship to study in Nigeria. He supplemented that study abroad experience with readings and with his parents' memories of the Nigerian civil war during the late 1960s. Significantly, however, the narrative voices that speak to us in all three narratives are, by turn, cynical and confessional, and they constantly draw our attention to their own unreliability.

The three novels I analyze in chapter 5 use dystopic settings and images to convey their protagonists' trauma. *Moses, Citizen, and Me* (by Sierra Leonean–British writer Delia Jarrett-Macauley), *Half of a Yellow Sun* (by Nigerian-American novelist Chimamanda Adichie), and *Song for Night* (by Nigerian-British novelist Chris Abani), present the child in combat in nightmarish ways. In *Moses, Citizen, and Me,* protagonist Julia can only imagine the lives of Sierra Leonean child soldiers like Citizen by having them inhabit, literally, the inside of her head. By contrast, *Half of a Yellow Sun* focuses mostly on the ways in which civilian women, like protagonist Olanna, coped during the Nigerian-Biafran war. When the war itself appears in the narrative, it seems surreal. Child soldier Ugwu's brief combat experience is like Mene's: he is confused and isolated and has nightmares about violence against women. Several events are left unexplained, and even at the end, we are left guessing about how much of the narrative is to be trusted (since Ugwu's version of the war, explained in his own words, is yet to be written). The dead child soldier My Luck, the protagonist of *Song for Night,* exists in a sort of life-in-death limbo, invisible to humans but capable of suffering pain and hunger, and also calls attention to his own unreliability as a narrator. The emphasis in these three novels on dystopic, nightmarish events differentiates them from the fragmented, ambiguous narratives of *Beasts of No Nation, Allah Is Not Obliged,* and *Johnny Mad Dog.*

The Testimonial

The narrative uncertainty that is embedded within many African child soldier narratives makes them contradictory texts, texts that are marked by differences from differences, whose heterogeneous structures also contain elements that annihilate them (Derrida 98). In this regard, they are different from texts that are often used in the public domain as testimonials of endurance. A testimonial, according to John Beverley, is a form of life writing that affirms "the individual self *in a collective mode*" (29). Philip Holden has calls the testimonial a "sophisticated transcultural form that rephrases marginalized experiences and worldviews within a narrative form familiar to those who live in metropolitan capitalist societies" (123). One of the more well-known "testimonials of endurance" was Guatemalan activist and Nobel Peace Prize winner Rigoberta Menchú's memoir, *I, Rigoberta Menchú* (1983, 1984). *I, Rigoberta Menchú* did, formally speaking, "rephrase" the experiences of the Quiché (Mayan) Indians in Guatemala within a traditional storytelling form. Even as it did so, critics claimed it was not an "eyewitness account" of their struggles, despite its claims to be as much. Both the writing process (how Argentinian journalist Elisabeth Burgos-Debray put the narrative together) and the subject matter (whether or not the violence took place in the manner described) came under fire. The story was written down by Burgos-Debray in 1982 in France, via a series of taped interviews with Menchú and other Quiché (Mayan) activists (Arias 6). Menchú was illiterate and was not fluent in Spanish. One of the more noteworthy incidents Menchú described to Burgos-Debray was the brutal murder of her brother, Petrocinio. That incident appears in chapter 14, in which Menchú, along with some of her family members, notice that Petrocinio's "head was shaved and slashed. He had no [finger]nails. He had no soles to his feet . . . [he was] missing part of the tongue" (Menchú 208). As they watch, he is doused with gasoline and set on fire (209). In chapter 27, Menchú's mother is cut to pieces and dies of exposure "in terrible agony" (234). When Burgos-Debray represented these and other gruesome incidents in the book, she rearranged the chapters so that a form of chronology would emerge (Holden 123). By 1986, partly due to circulation of the book and partly due to shifting alliances within the various guerrilla groups, Menchú became an international celebrity (10), winning the Nobel Peace Prize in 1992. The memoir thereby became what Schaffer and Smith call a "symbol of the revolutionary spirit and struggle of a people" (Schaffer and Smith 30).[6]

Sixteen years after *I, Rigoberta Menchú* was published, David Stoll, an American anthropologist, wrote a book about Menchú entitled *Rigoberta Menchú and the Story of All Poor Guatemalans* (1999) in which he claimed that several of the important incidents in the book (such as the murders of Petrocinio and Rigoberta's mother, described above) could not have been witnessed by Menchú herself and may not even have taken place. That in turn generated a huge media controversy (Holden 123). Within the United States, readers and activities fiercely debated the "authenticity" of the memoir, and questioned the nature of truth telling (Schaffer and Smith 30). Stoll's accusations and the media coverage that followed caused both the plight of the Quiché Indians and the testimonial genre itself to be contested.

As the controversy surrounding *I, Rigoberta Menchú* suggests, testimonial-style memoirs, especially those that use linear narrative structures, can often be regarded, in the public domain, as factual accounts of endurance rather than contradictory narratives about agency in the face of adversity. African child soldier narratives use dystopic imagery and affective registers to describe how African children in combat build resilience against ongoing oppressive situations. Such narratives create contradictory and ambiguous forms of agency for their protagonists. The extent of agency exhibited by real child soldiers has been influenced, to a large extent, by changing notions of trauma within clinical and academic circles. Although it was well known, by the mid-twentieth century, that combat trauma affected "every aspect of soldiers' lives, including their physical health, social wellbeing,

economic standards, cultural outlooks, and political attitudes"
(Krippner and McIntyre 6–7), late twentieth-century definitions
of trauma tended to focus on how acts of traumatic remembering
were often "fitful, incomplete, and belated" (Schaffer and Smith
20). Cathy Caruth, Geoffrey Hartman, and Dominick LaCapra
analyzed texts that were written about traumatic experiences,
and Caruth argued that textual indeterminacies or paradoxes gave
readers unique access to traumatic events, which would otherwise
not be representable (45).[7] Caruth suggested that traumatic events
are inherently incomprehensible and can only be articulated after
the fact, in a "belated" or "delayed" fashion (8). Therefore, the act
of constructing linear chronological narratives about traumatic
events is, in her view, extremely challenging. In the twenty-first
century, however, earlier notions of trauma, with their focus on
the Holocaust as the emblematic example, and of fragmented
narratives as exemplary were challenged. Scientifically speaking,
the notion that trauma causes amnesia or dissociation, or can only
be understood after the fact, was questioned. Richard McNally
argued that trauma does not always cause amnesia or dissociation,
and that high levels of stress hormones do not necessarily impair
memories of the traumatic event (190). He suggested that the
fact that trauma survivors frequently did not dwell on their past
trauma has little to do with their inability to remember it (193).
Therefore, the reluctance of trauma survivors to describe their
experiences came to be regarded as the result of choice rather
than ability (Pedersen 334). McNally used the term "peritraumatic
dissociation," or "dissociative alterations in consciousness," to
describe the narrative distortions used by trauma survivors, such
as their sense that during the trauma time was slowing down or
that everything appeared unreal (93). He suggested that trauma
survivors can, in fact, describe their traumatizing events; and that
even if they alter some of the narrative details, this does not mean

that they cannot remember the events themselves (McNally 184).
Judith Butler, Derek Summerfield, and Ethan Watters argued that
Caruth and others frequently ignored the trauma experienced by
non-Western cultures or minority groups; that they universalized
Western notions of trauma; and that they were prescriptive in their
preference for aesthetic practices that used "fragmentation and
aporia" to represent trauma (Craps, "Beyond Eurocentrism" 46).
Schaffer and Smith argued that Western trauma theorists' focus
on the individual survivor who remembers past trauma and then
writes about it "universalizes diverse and multiple structures of
feelings, eliding gender, racial, and ethnic differences" (22) and
also fails to address the larger "genealogies and architectures of
cultural memory" (23). Summerfield and Watters pointed out
(using examples) that uncritical application of Western notions of
trauma in non-Western cultures and situations is harmful (Craps,
"Beyond Eurocentrism" 48). Stef Craps suggested that in many
analyses about trauma, even those that involved Africans and other
non-Europeans, empathy is "surreptitiously redirected toward the
European character [under examination], and the non-European
other ends up being silenced, excluded from the empathy loop,
his or her suffering ignored" ("Not Closing Loop" 57). Derek
Summerfield argued that in many instances, even in Europe, war
trauma is not regarded solely as a mental health issue ("Medicalization of Suffering" 241).

Ananya Kabir advocated analyzing what she calls "affect clus-
ters" or "different expressive registers" about trauma, including
song and dance, which exist alongside more traditional registers
(66). In calling attention to expressive registers, Kabir underscores
what anthropologists like Rosalind Shaw have also shown, that
traumatic memories (such as modern Sierra Leoneans' memories
of the slave trade) often surface indirectly via "memoryscapes"
(images and social practices remembered communally), including

oral narratives about apocalypses that transform the landscape, or about dangerous, marauding spirits that roam invisibly in a magical landscape, harming people (Shaw 56). Temne religious practices, for example, changed as a result of the traumas of the slave trade, and these modifications reflected the historical transformations brought about by the Atlantic slave trade (50–62). Other trauma critics, like Stef Craps, have suggested that trauma, especially in non-Western cultures, frequently arises, not from a single, catastrophic event (like the Holocaust) but rather, from everyday, ongoing forms of oppression and powerlessness that are systemic and difficult to alleviate ("Beyond Eurocentrism" 50–51). On the one hand, a person who is in fear of constant harassment at a workplace that otherwise seems quite safe can experience trauma-like symptoms, which get triggered by the "unpredictability and invisibility of potential perpetrators" (Brown 98). On the other hand, a person who has experienced horrendous events may have recourse to some kind of "inner force" that builds up resilience and enables him or her to recover without heavy reliance on medication (Akhtar and Wrenn 5). As the following chapters will demonstrate, African child soldier narratives, with their emphasis on the ambiguous agency of their protagonists, underscore the numerous ways in which children encounter traumatic situations and find ways to resist them.

Children and Wars in Africa

The "everyday trauma" experienced by child soldiers in Africa often continued well after the hostilities were over. Sociologists and historians like Alcinda Honwana (2006), Peter Eichstaedt (2009), Myriam Denov (2010), Opiyo Oloya (2013), and Susan Shepler (2014) have studied the role that child combatants played in specific conflicts in Africa, such as those in Uganda and Sierra Leone. Alcinda Honwana's important study, *Child Soldiers in Africa* (2006), focused on the involvement of children in wars in Angola and Mozambique from the 1970s onward. Honwana did extensive fieldwork in both countries with child combatants, sexually abused girls, children living in military camps, and children victimized by armed groups. She concluded that modern warfare techniques significantly impacted the experiences of child soldiers in southern Africa, despite which they retained a sense of agency and could be successfully rehabilitated (3–4). Myriam Denov's *Child Soldiers: Sierra Leone's Revolutionary United Front* (2010) provided an excellent analysis of the conditions that led children to become involved in war, with a particular focus on the role that child soldiers played in Sierra Leone's 1991–2002 civil war. Her analysis was based on the extensive fieldwork she did with former child soldiers there, and she examined the various processes that resulted in both their militarization and demilitarization. She argued that rather than being either "extreme victims, extreme perpetrators or extreme heroes" the children's identities were instead "messy, ambiguous and paradoxical," and that it was precisely these indeterminacies that led to considerable challenges "in their post-conflict lives" (2). She also suggested that media and academic narratives about child soldiers have tended to be so stereotypical that the children have become, in her words, "pathologized" into some kind of perversion of innocence and purity (7). The degree to which traumatized individuals are influenced by media and other outside narratives about them has been discussed at length by trauma theorists. Derek Summerfield and others have shown that social attitudes do influence the narratives of people experiencing trauma, to the extent that they help "shape what individual victims feel has been done to them, and shape the vocabulary they use to describe this ... societally constructed ideas about outcomes ... carry a measure of self-fulfilling prophecy" (234). Therefore, former child soldiers writing about their experiences may indeed shape their narratives around socially accepted norms and stereotypes.

This groundbreaking analysis, by social scientists and academics, of the sociocultural contexts surrounding child soldiers in Africa was complemented by the scholarship of legal and military experts like Tim Allen (2006), Michael Wessells (2009), Roméo Dallaire (2011), and Mark Drumbl (2012), which focused on the role of political and judicial structures in mediating global conflicts and adjudicating punishment. Tim Allen's *Trial Justice: The International Criminal Court and the Lord's Resistance Army* (2006) focused on the disconnect between systems of international criminal justice and the realities faced by the survivors of Uganda's Lord's Resistance Army (LRA). Allen analyzed the impact of the activities of the LRA on the Acholi people of northern Uganda, among whom he did extensive field research. Allen not only provides an excellent historical summary of the rise of Joseph Kony and the LRA but also shows how international institutions dealing with criminal justice issues can, in fact, undermine local and well-established sociolegal justice systems. Allen's insights about the undermining of justice in Uganda have been echoed by legal scholar Jennifer Moore, who points out that International Criminal Court indictments of senior LRA leaders "without any parallel war crimes indictments of government soldiers in international or domestic Ugandan courts have raised the specter of differential treatment in Uganda's approach to transitional justice" (215). Moore argues that in Uganda, as in many parts of sub-Saharan Africa, concepts of justice are both retributive and restorative, with social and economic, as well as criminal and legal, aspects (216, 198). Therefore, institutions and approaches toward justice should include both international and local ones, such as truth commissions and cleansing ceremonies. She cites as one example *mato oput,* a cleansing ceremony during which perpetrators are accepted back within communities they have harmed (216–218). Somewhat on the same lines, internationally known UN military commander-turned-diplomat Roméo Dallaire argued, in *They Fight Like Soldiers, They Die Like Children* (2011) that children in many African countries around the world are sometimes used as "portable weapon systems" because they are cheap, renewable, and expendable. His preferred solutions to end the use of children in combat involve a combination of military and diplomatic efforts, such as those practiced by his own nongovernmental agency (NGO), the Child Soldiers Initiative, which successfully brought together military members, ex-child soldiers, NGOs, and academics.

Literary critics like Pius Ngandu Nkashama (2003), Odile Cazenave (2005), James Dawes (2009), Roger Berger (2010), Alexandra Schultheis (2010), Jack Kearney (2010), Anne Whitehead (2011), and Mark Sanders (2011) have analyzed specific narratives and memoirs written about child soldiers. Berger's important article "Decolonizing African Autobiography" makes important points about the uniqueness of African life writing. He argues that the African autobiography has shifted from the tragic to the comic mode and is able to negotiate variations in history, language, genre, time, and politics. Sanders, in his article "Culpability and Guilt: Child Soldiers in Fiction and Memoir," argues that when child soldiers are made to believe they aren't culpable for their violent actions, that assessment contradicts their inner feelings of guilt. He also suggests that fiction and autobiography (like Ahmadou Kourouma's *Allah Is Not Obliged,* Melanie Klein's *Narrative of a Child Analysis,* and Ishmael Beah's *A Long Way Gone)* can help actual children who have committed violent acts gain more insights about their actions during combat. However, how much help the narratives actually provide to former child soldiers is debatable given the lack of opportunities child soldiers have to read such texts. Since *Allah Is Not Obliged* is a very different narrative than *A Long Way Gone,* both stylistically and formally, Sanders's comments suggest that their differences are less important than their outreach to other former child soldiers. Given the struggles former child soldiers have to go through in order to get their voices heard (described in more detail in chapters 2 and 3), their outreach efforts have been fairly limited. Although Beah has been involved in personal outreach work, this may not have done more than provide the financial means for more outreach work.

Scholars of life writing and literary critics such as Philippe Lejeune (1989), Timothy Neale (2010), Sidonie Smith (2010), and Alexandra Moore and Elizabeth Goldberg (2015) have theorized about the connections and disconnections between factual and imaginative truths within memoirs and autobiographies. In this regard, much attention has been paid to testimonies about the Holocaust, including the controversy surrounding the fake Holocaust survivor memoir *Fragments: Memories of a Childhood, 1939–1948,* by Binjamin Wilkomirski. *Fragments* had a trajectory similar to that of Menchú's memoir, but with different results.[8] Wilkomirski was born Bruno Grosjean and took the name of his Swiss adoptive parents, Dössekker. In 1995, he published a memoir entitled *Bruchstücke* (known in English as *Fragments*), which was translated into nine languages and became recognized as a "major testimony about the Nazi era" (Neale 432). Its narrative structure consisted of a series of fragmented images loosely connected, which supposedly represented his traumatized memory. It included details about Nazi medical experimentations and the brutalities that occurred at Auschwitz, and it eventually won several awards. In 1998, a Holocaust survivor named Daniel Ganzfried investigated what he thought were inconsistencies in the narrative and concluded that Wilkomirski had never been in a

Nazi concentration camp. In 1999, historian Stefan Maechler also investigated the issue and, in a book published in 2001 named *The Wilkomirski Affair,* confirmed Ganzfried's conclusions. Ganzfried and Maechler proved that Wilkomirski had never been either in Latvia (where he had claimed he was born) or in Poland (where he had claimed he was in a concentration camp) during World War II and was not a Holocaust survivor. Ganzfried called Wilkomirski a liar, Maechler labeled *Fragments* a fraud, and by 1999 it was taken out of print (Hungerford 67). Blake Eskin, an American of Latvian Jewish descent, wrote a book entitled *A Life in Pieces: The Making and Unmaking of Binjamin Wilkomirski* in 2002, which corroborated the findings of both Ganzfried and Maechler (Walford 118). Other critics, among them Elena Lappin and Philip Gourevitch, argued that Wilkomirski wasn't so much a liar as a deluded person (Hungerford 67).

What is of interest to literary critics about the Wilkomirski affair is the fact that Wilkomirski did in fact have a traumatic childhood (he was an orphan brought up by foster parents) and had used some of his childhood experiences, together with his conversations with actual Holocaust survivors, to write his fake testimony (Neale 432). Timothy Neale suggests that Wilkomirski may have had cynical reasons for presenting himself as what he was not; however, his fake narrative underscores the "conditional" nature of testimony itself, a form of storytelling that is based on "substitution, elaboration, and adaptation" (Neale 444). My purpose, in this book, is not to debate the factual veracity, or lack thereof, within narratives written by and about African child soldiers. Instead, I will describe the ways in which the ambiguity within the form and content of the African child soldier narrative simultaneously connects and disconnects them from their readers. Dystopic imagery, ambiguous narratives, and strange aporias enable these narratives to draw attention to the trauma experienced by African children in unique ways. Near the end of *Sozaboy,* the child soldier protagonist Mene laments that everyone he knows has died and that the few remaining survivors don't really understand why they have been fighting so long (112). Confusing, traumatic losses like those experienced by Mene create tensions within these narratives that are often hard to unravel. Yet such tensions are often productive because, as Moore and Goldberg suggest, "demands for legal certainty in the form of human rights claims often emerge out of narrative and historical ambiguity" (4). As the following chapters will show, African child soldier novels and memoirs, with their formal and stylistic ambiguities, are both productive and unsettling in unique ways.

CHAPTER 2

False Combat and Adolescent Life Writing

My eyes were burning and my mind was overloaded with conflicting instructions and emotions. I felt as much wild excitement as fear. In this moment, we were two warriors—he with his gun, me with mine—and I was still pulling long on the trigger. I could see my bullets chewing at the bricks, creating small explosions of dried mud as they went. . . . Suddenly, I was on my back in the mud with the rain still falling on me. . . . My chest burned as if it was on fire, but I couldn't put it out.

—Romeo Dallaire, *They Fight Like Soldiers,
They Die Like Children*

"Narratives," Ethiopian novelist Dinaw Mengestu once wrote, are "the bastard children of war—the indirect and necessary products of violence. In the absence of a narrative voice, we are left only with anecdotes, body counts and haunting images that we can never fully explain. Africa has had enough of these" (61). Are narratives written by former child soldiers byproducts of the violence itself? As I have shown in my previous chapter, child soldiers in Africa or elsewhere are not a recent phenomenon. Militias and military forces around the world have recruited children as young as seven ever since wars have existed. However, until recently, very few of those children wrote about their experiences, and even fewer tried to publish their writings. Three fairly well-known war memoirs about child soldiers in Africa not only depict how such stories are the "bastard children of war" but also how profoundly contradictory these narratives can be. They are Ugandan-Danish China Keitetsi's *Child Soldier: Fighting for My Life* (2002 in Danish, 2004 in English); Eritrean-German Senait Mehari's *Heart of Fire: One Girl's Extraordinary Journey from Child Soldier to Soul Singer* (2004 in German, 2006 in English); and Sierra Leonean–American Ishmael Beah's *A Long Way Gone: Memoirs of a Child Soldier* (2007 in English).

All three memoirs were written by former child soldiers using chronological narratives referencing actual combat experiences, and unfolding within public spheres experiencing flux. As Joseph Slaughter has shown, the modern European public sphere was created alongside the modern nation-state in the eighteenth century. Associated with the notion of the "general will," it was linked to the idea that European citizens were in possession of certain human rights (146). This public sphere had regulatory functions that determined what formal elements could be used in personal narratives written by such citizens (146). The six African child soldier memoirs under analysis in this chapter and the next, like numerous European bildungsromans before them, not only tell the stories of their protagonists' socialization processes, but also depict the situations that result when "the modern institutional guarantors of social order and meaning . . . have been perverted" (Slaughter 150). The six narratives are complex and ambivalent, using binary oppositions and contradictory imagery as they narrate how their protagonists overcame violence and trauma. These narrative ambiguities both connect and disconnect with their reading publics in unexpected ways.

Child Soldier, A Long Way Gone, and *Heart of Fire* adhere to
the broad outlines of traditional Western definitions of the autobiography, being "retrospective prose narrative[s]" written by
real people with an emphasis on the evolution of the protagonist's
personality (Lejeune 4). At the same time, there are ambiguous
and contradictory twists within these narratives. Some of these
ambiguities arise from the conflicted relationships between the
speaking voices within these memoirs and the public domains
within which they unfold. Writing about South African outlaw
Dugmore Boetie's 1969 autobiography, *Familiarity Is the Kingdom
of the Lost,* Roger A. Berger suggests that it "both chronicles the
life of an out-law and violates the . . . 'autobiographical pact' between autobiographer and reader . . . [it] both praises and debunks
the autobiography" (40). Speaking voices that reflect tensions
between authors and subjects also exist in other disciplines, such
as journalism. Janet Malcolm's *The Journalist and the Murderer*
(1990), for example, traces the fascinating story, unfolding in the
United States in the 1980s, of a lawsuit filed by convicted (and
jailed) murderer Jeffrey MacDonald against journalist Joe Mc-
Ginnis, whose *Fatal Vision* argued that MacDonald had killed his
family in a fit of drug-induced rage. The problem was that McGinnis had written the book over a period of four years with a lot of
cooperation from the jailed MacDonald, who had fully believed
that McGinnis would present him as an innocent scapegoat. The
lawsuit resulted in McGinnis going to jail. As Malcolm puts it, "An
abyss lies between the journalist's experience of being out in the
world talking to people and his experience of being alone in a room
writing" (59–60). The same could be said of life-writers. While
not all memoirists would agree with Malcolm that "the writer of
non-fiction is under contract to the reader to limit himself to events
that actually occurred . . . he may not embellish the truth about
these events or these characters" (153), the speaking voices within

memoirs are conflicted in various ways. William L. Andrews, writing about Olaudah Equiano's famous 1789 autobiography, *The Interesting Narrative of the Life of Olaudah Equiano, or Gustavus Vassa, the African,* argues that he was "not the innocent African as sacrificial lamb . . . nor . . . the outraged African as shorn and dishonored lion. . . . He was both—he was neither. He was outsider and insider and somewhere on the margin in between" (60). The "I"s that speak within the pages of *Child Soldier, Heart of Fire,* and *A Long Way Gone* speak both as adults and as children, and represent themselves as both citizens and exiles. The complexities of these speaking voices mark them off against early modern European notions of childhood. As Sharon Stephens points out, even into the twentieth century, children were often regarded, by European experts, as helpless subjects in need of "protection and enculturation" (10); therefore, adult anger and retribution were sanctioned against children who could not or would not conform to their expected roles (11). Children who behaved differently were often measured, by adults, against "universalized notions of an ideal childhood" (16). By "universalized," of course, Stephens means early modern European constructions of childhood, which, together with concepts of gender, race, and nature, were greatly influenced by "European colonialist experiences" (18). The three memoirs under discussion in this chapter offer no such "universalized" notions of childhood, presenting it instead in complex and nuanced ways. These complex depictions also reflect the realities on the ground in many parts of Africa where, as social scientists suggest, political violence, economic collapses, and disease epidemics have "created a crisis of unprecedented proportions for younger generations of Africans" (de Boeck and Honwana 1).

All three memoirs were written after their authors emigrated, or began to live, in the West. Being, thus, migrants and then immigrant writers, their speaking voices occupy a liminal space. As

Homi Bhabha has indicated, "Migrants, refugees, and nomads don't merely circulate. They need to settle, claim asylum or nationality, demand housing and education, assert their economic and cultural rights, and come to be legally represented" (n.p.). China Keitetsi, Senait Mehari, and Ishmael Beah use linear, first-person narratives to describe the trauma they experienced as they moved from place to place, finally emigrating to Europe or America. However, their narratives also reflect a variety of expectations and desires that they experienced in each place. All three narratives use literary and rhetorical devices in order to "contest and sometimes even subvert the imagined world of the official mind ... that surrounds them" (Appadurai 329).

The three memoirs subvert official versions of life in war zones in numerous ways. China Keitetsi, author of *Child Soldier: Fighting for My Life,* has been described as the "first former African girl soldier to have written about her experiences" ("Women and Gender" 1). Keitetsi's first-person narrative is full of descriptions of various kinds of combat, starting with her childhood in rural western Uganda in the 1970s, when she resisted her abusive father and stepmother, themselves refugees from Rwanda (Keitetsi, interview). Among other details, the narrator mentions that "China" was Keitetsi's nom de guerre, her real name being Jacqueline, and that when she was only six months old, her father divorced her mother and separated her from Keitetsi, as punishment for not producing a son (Keitetsi, *Child Soldier* 1). So Keitetsi grew up partly on her grandmother's farm and partly with her father and stepmother. Everyone, from her violent father to her vindictive stepmother and her cruel grandmother, abused her (2–51).

Most of the narrative focuses on Keitetsi's adolescent years during the early 1980s, when she joined the ranks of the National Resistance Army (NRA), a rebel group led by (now president) Yoweri Museveni, as it fought against then-president Milton

Obote's Uganda National Liberation Army (UNLA). The narrator mentions that when Keitetsi was eight years old she ran away and joined the NRA, and was brutalized and traumatized through its various conflicts with the UNLA (114–126). Even after the conflict was over and Museveni became president, Keitetsi was abused and raped, and eventually, after a brief stay in South Africa during which she was raped and attacked, she emigrated to Denmark (268). Her Danish friends (specifically a social worker) encouraged her to write down her traumatic memories, as a way of helping her cope, and that was published as *Mit Liv Som Barnesoldat I Uganda*. When I interviewed her, Keitetsi indicated that she wrote the memoir in English, but that it was translated into Danish before being published in 2002 by Ekstra Bladet in Copenhagen ("Spotlight"). According to its website, Ekstra Bladet is part of JP Politiken publishing house and publishes books on current events, crime, and politics, among others, valuing a "sharp angle and a good story" ("About Ekstra Bladet"). Two years after its Danish publication, it appeared in English and was also translated into several other languages, including German. It became a bestseller in Germany (Foster 12), where it was entitled *Sie nahmen mir die Mutter und gaben mir ein Gewehr* (*They Took Away My Mother and Gave Me a Gun*) (Swart).

In her foreword Keitetsi tells us that her main reason for writing was not to subvert official narratives about the war. Rather, it was therapeutic, aiming, as she put it, to empty herself "of the stones that I could feel breaking my shoulders" (x). Weeping as she wrote, she found that the memoir helped her to become a "normal child" again (x). She seems to have written it in seclusion, and her grammar and syntax are somewhat idiosyncratic. She did get some help from a copyeditor provided by her publishing company (Keitetsi, interview). The success of the memoir seems to have made her a celebrity of sorts, and Nelson Mandela actually wrote a poem about her (Keitetsi, *Child Soldier* x). She eventually became an activist on behalf of child soldiers while also working as a kindergarten assistant in Denmark, and later set up a safe house in Rwanda for girl victims of abuse (Foster 12).

Despite the memoir's success in international circles, it was condemned by Ugandan authorities, who roundly disputed Keitetsi's claim that current president (and then NRA commander) Yoweri Museveni actively recruited child soldiers. The Ugandan government reacted even more negatively to a documentary film by CNN about Keitetsi's life, directed by South African journalist Susan Puren, and entitled *China, War Child* (1995). In that film, Puren suggested that the NRA was guilty of atrocities against children. In response, the Ugandan government accused Keitetsi of being a liar and a thief (Atuhaire, "Keitetsi Tours"). Arguing that the NRA actually looked after its soldiers well, especially since they were either orphaned or abandoned, the Museveni government claimed that the NRA provided its soldiers with jobs and livelihoods (Boyd). It also accused Keitetsi of perpetrating a hoax in order to "gain sympathy and secure asylum" abroad, and of stealing millions of Ugandan shillings (Nakazibwe). According to government records, Keitetsi was seventeen, not eight, when she became a soldier (Atuhaire, "War Videos"). In May 2003, the government released its own documentary, *Child Soldiers, The Media Hoax* to counter Keitetsi's claims that girl soldiers were severely abused by the NRA (Wasike). This video depicts Keitetsi as not just a liar and a thief but also a human trafficker, claiming that she sold off her own children in South Africa (Kameo). While it is difficult to verify every detail of Keitetsi's story, her storyline does fit the broad outlines of narratives provided by other child soldiers worldwide (Boyd). Moreover, it does seem apparent that girls and minors were abused by the NRA between the years 1981 and 1986. Keitetsi has responded to these claims by Ugandan authorities by pointing out that Museveni tends to attack those who say negative things about him because he wants to stay in power (Keitetsi, interview).

The factual accuracy of Keitetsi's memoir is less important than its narrative style. The narrative persona is contradictory, and its agency constantly shifts. As Laura Brown argues, human identities, even in nontraumatic situations, are multiple and contradictory; therefore traumatized human identities, when they intersect with existing identities, often produce unexpected outcomes (17). In some instances, Brown argues, trauma manifests itself in "quotidian" ways, and the flashbacks or numbness that trauma survivors experience are coping strategies rather than manifestations of illness (18). In one scene in *Child Soldier,* the narrator describes how Keitetsi is forced to cope with the realization that her fellow child soldiers are actually battle-hardened murderers. She writes: "It was strange to see most other children having a kind of lust for killing and torturing. . . . It annoyed me that I always had to feel sorry for others, even the enemy. I had crossed the line. . . . Now it was time to decide, from being a broken, but kind and unselfish individual, to being a full-blooded killer, if I only could" (134–135). The narrative voice here suggests that because the young Keitetsi cannot turn herself into a killing machine, she is forced to cover up her true feelings and, like the other child soldiers, experiences revulsion and confusion: "The sound was terrifyingly loud and everything on the road seemed to splinter into pieces as rocket-propelled grenades (RPGs) hit the trucks. I was more frightened than ever . . . [and] I was getting confused, having been told that I was fighting for freedom, but I had never imagined that to include stealing from the dead" (117). Not only is she (and her fellow child soldiers) encouraged to kill and then loot from the dead, but she is also instructed to be cruel to the living: "We would increase our brutality towards our prisoners just to gain more ranks. . . . But we were too young to realise that our actions . . . would haunt our dreams and thoughts for ever" (124). It is noteworthy that here the narrator inserts adult insights about the lingering effect of trauma on her life, while also describing an overwhelming sense of confusion and pain.

One aspect of Keitetsi's narrative that is significant is her use of repetition. Many scenes and images reflect each other. One narrative repetition is that of escape and return, or sequences during which Keitetsi escapes from her unit, only to return to it or a similar unit soon after. For example, in one scene, the young Keitetsi runs away from her unit and makes her way back to her father's house. Full of anger and hatred, she takes along her big army rifle, with the intention of killing her abusive father, but she loses her nerve at the last minute (143). This scene looks back to episodes that the narrator had mentioned earlier on, in which the young Keitetsi had resigned herself to being constantly beaten by her father for very trivial offenses, such as for eating the bananas growing on his farm (33) or for wetting her bed at night (65). It also links to another escape scene earlier in the narrative when Keitetsi had run away from her unit and had gone looking for her biological mother, from whom she had been separated in infancy. After considerable difficulty, she locates her mother's house and is overjoyed to be reunited with her. However, rather than stay and get to know her mother better, she abruptly leaves, terrified that the feast her happy mother is preparing for her will kill her. As the narrator tells us in an aside, Keitetsi was convinced that her mother was going to put her into her cooking pot and devour her! (111).

Besides repeating scenes in which Keitetsi escapes conflicts only to return to them, the narrative of *Child Soldier* also focuses on Keitetsi's tendency to constantly reinvent her identity. In one scene, Keitetsi realizes that it wasn't just her fear of being eaten that had prompted her to run away from her mother's house; it was also her apprehensions about becoming a civilian again. When her sisters suggest that she go back to school, she has deep misgivings. She writes: "Suddenly I realised that I would have to start all over with my life, if I wanted to make it . . . I simply didn't fit into this community, being a small girl with a vast military experience. I hardly knew anything but the ways of a soldier" (147). Several scenes later, however, Keitetsi rejects that same knowledge of "the ways of a soldier" when she realizes that her new training camp (for recruits) is much worse than any situation she encountered at home. She is horrified to learn, but narrates in a matter-of-fact way, that she, along with the other girl soldiers, is expected to "offer sex to more than five officers in one unit, and to those of lower ranks . . . every day in the week, we had to sleep with different *afandes* [commanders] against our will! If we refused . . . we would have to say goodbye to our family" (155–156). Unsurprisingly, the young Keitetsi solves this situation just like she solves her other situations, namely, by "disappearing" again.

The narrative of the later part of the memoir is filled with descriptions of various kinds of disappearing acts (159–161), several of which focus on how Keitetsi moves from one job, such as presidential palace guard (165), to another, such as bodyguard to Officer Ahmed Kashilingi (171). With each job change, her personality transforms itself, too, until unexpectedly, she evolves into a loving mother. These rapid changes in Keitetsi's personality, as reflected in the narrative, seem less a result of her age (she was still an adolescent) than a product of her living in proximity to violence. She writes: "Now I had a child who I loved more than anything else. . . . Most of us [other girl soldiers who were mothers] were too young to be mothers, but in the NRA there was no age. . . . Too many young mothers had to figure out how to be both mothers and fathers" (210). Many misadventures later, after she migrates to Denmark, she imagines she is living "at the end of the world. .... This world I had come to had been as an image of heaven before, and I was surprised to see that not everything was so" (269–270). This imagery of a new life located at the "end of the world" underscores what the narrative has already shown, namely, that Keitetsi survives by constantly reinventing herself. The narrative focus of Senait Mehari's *Heart of Fire,* like that of *Child Soldier,* is centered on Mehari's evolving sense of agency as she is forced to fight with the Eritrean Liberation Front (ELF) in its war of independence from Ethiopia. The first-person narrator describes, in linear fashion, how the infant Mehari, abandoned by her parents, grows up, for the first six years of her life, first in an orphanage and then with her grandparents. In 1979, when she turns six, her father, Ghebrehiwet, "sells" her to the ELF, along with her two half-sisters, Yaldiyan and Tzegehana (Mehari 53–54). At that time, the ELF was fighting on two fronts: against the Ethiopian army and against its rival, the Eritrean People's Liberation Front (EPLF) (56). Mehari narrates how she and her sisters remain child soldiers with the ELF for three years, during which time they are often starved, beaten, and raped. Mehari is saved from going to the front only because she doesn't have the strength to lift an AK-47. In 1981, Ghebrehiwet sends his brother, Haile, to rescue the three girls, and they live with Haile in Khartoum, Sudan. In 1987, the supposedly penitent Ghebrehiwet, who has by now emigrated to Germany, sends for them and they move to Hamburg (Didcock). When Ghebrehiwet begins to abuse the fourteen-year-old Mehari, she runs away from home. After living on the streets of Hamburg, she begins to write music, eventually becoming a successful pop singer (Didcock).

After making a name for herself as a singer, Mehari wrote her memoir, in German, a language in which she is fluent, and in 2004 it was published as *Feuerherz,* by Droemer. Droemer Verlag is part of the Droemer Knaur, and Holtzbrinck and Weltbild publishing corporation. Under the editorship of Willy Droemer, it has, since World War II, published best sellers by such prominent authors as Normal Mailer and James Michener ("Verlagsgruppe Droemer Knaur"). In the United States and the United Kingdom, Macmillan manages and distributes its books ("About"). In an interview, Mehari claimed that she wrote the memoir because a German newspaper once referred to her as a killer (Didcock). She also wanted to make Europeans understand "what a typical childhood in Africa can be like and what it means to be a child soldier. . . . Germany was so shocked about my story but there are millions of kids just like me in Africa. It's still happening" (Didcock). She took the opportunity to deny that she had ever killed anyone (Didcock), and to state that for her, as it was for Keitetsi, the writing of the memoir was partly therapeutic. She mentions in the narrative that until she turned sixteen she had refused to tell anyone about her traumatic experiences. She had become suicidal and had had to undergo six years of therapy and counseling before she was able to talk about it even with her half-sisters (Didcock). After the therapy, she went to Ethiopia to meet her mother, Adhanet, and soon after their reunion Adhanet died of an illness. After the memoir was published, Mehari's father, Ghebrehiwet, read it and was very moved by it. "The imprint of my past," Mehari indicates in an interview, "is still with me and I cannot truly fit in until I have fully come to terms with it. Until then, I will constantly swing between my old and my new selves" (Millard).

In her epilogue, Mehari tells us a bit more about those "old" and "new" selves. After Droemer Verlag published *Feuerherz,* her life changed dramatically. Publicly, she gained a lot of media attention and was interviewed by local radio and TV outlets (Mehari 253). On a personal level, she was reunited, on a visit to Addis Ababa, Ethiopia, with Luul, her long-lost brother (253). This was before she was reunited with her mother. On her return to Germany she worked for UNICEF, and her book was translated into seven or eight European languages (254). Christine Lo did the English translation. The German edition and the translations together sold nearly half a million copies worldwide ("Controversial Child Soldier Film"). On the more negative side, however, members of the Eritrean community in Germany accused her of making up things.

Mehari summarizes their objections, in her epilogue, as unsupported assertions claiming that child soldiers were never used by either side in the Ethiopian-Eritrean war, nor had there been any famine in Eritrea (254). She refutes these assertions by stating that German aid organizations had evidence that child soldiers had indeed been used by both sides in the war, and that there had, in fact, been a famine (254). However, Mehari's epilogue does not mention that an Eritrean woman named Almaz Yohannes had sued Mehari's publishers, Droemer Verlag, for libel, claiming that the book wrongfully depicted her as running a training center for child soldiers. Yohannes claimed she neither ran such a school nor ordered the executions of children, as Mehari claims in her memoir. In 2008, Yohannes settled out of court with Droemer, which issued a statement admitting that the memoir did contain major errors ("Eritrean Child Soldier Memoir"). This controversy was further complicated by Mehari's claims in interviews that she wrote the book in response to accusations that she had killed people. As it happens, the European and American reviews of the book were largely positive, one Australian reviewer indicating, for example, that Mehari was a "very good writer ... evocative, confessional yet detached and quite heart-wrenching, especially in earlier sections of the book" (Carroll).

In 2009, a movie version of the book was produced with Italian-born Luigi Falorgni directing it ("Eritrean Child Soldier Memoir"). Falorni indicated that he decided to make a movie version because he believed that Mehari's experiences were "an inspiration to tell a universal story about girls in war" ("Controversial Child Soldier Film"). However, the Eritrean government did not view the story that way. It opposed the project, disputing Mehari's claim that child soldiers had been used in its war of independence against Ethiopia. Although Falorni had begun shooting in Eritrea, he quickly moved the locale to a refugee camp in Nairobi, Kenya, home to the largest community of Eritreans outside of Eritrea ("Controversial Child Soldier Film"). Named *Heart of Fire,* the film used lay actors who spoke in Tigrinya, not German ("Controversial Child Soldier Film"), and it was screened at the Berlin Film Festival in 2008, alongside Emmanuel Jal's movie *War Child,* which I will discuss in the next chapter ("Eritrean Child Soldier Memoir"). Soon after, the family of the movie's ten-year-old lead actress, Letekidan Micael (in the movie she was named Awet), was granted asylum in Europe and Letekidan started attending school there (Clarke).

In the memoir, the persona created by Mehari, like the persona within *Child Soldier,* constantly reinvents herself. As an infant, Mehari takes an instant disliking to her father when she meets him for the first time at age six. That feeling deepens when she is forced to leave her loving grandparents and aunts and move in with his family (Mehari 37–38). The physical abuse starts soon after that. Like Keitetsi, Mehari gets beaten often by Ghebrehiwet for not working hard enough: "My father did not beat me merely as a matter of course, though, but with a directed vindictiveness, regardless of whether I had done anything wrong . . . he beat me until all resistance died. He only stopped when I lay whimpering on the floor, curled up in agony" (48). On one occasion, for reasons she is never able to comprehend, Ghebrehiwet hefts a big machete with which to chop her to pieces, but is prevented at the last minute by his wife, Werhid, who shouts that he could sell her to the "Jebha" (ELF) instead (50–51). And the very next day he takes her, with her two half-sisters, Yaldiyan and Tzegehana, to the ELF encampment and hands them over as new recruits (52–53).

When, in 1980, Mehari becomes a *tegaldety* (child soldier), she is six or seven years old (Mehari 54). The ELF she joins is on its last legs, losing ground to its rival, the EPLF, and it actually "collapsed" the following year (65). As a result, the ELF unit she is placed with is in disarray. The early part of the narrative shows that Mehari is forced to learn new coping strategies on a daily basis. She regularly experiences extreme hunger and thirst, making her life "miserable" (59). Forced to keep changing the way she responds to her environment, she realizes that death is "everywhere" (75). In one scene, she jumps into a river to swim, lands on a bloodied corpse, and goes on to discover dozens more. As if the gut-wrenching sight of those corpses weren't enough, she is given the chore (along with a dozen other children) of pulling them out of the river, one by one: "We now had to dig them out of the riverbed and drag them up. . . . The sweetish, repellent smell of death and decay spread around the river and toward the camp, settling upon it like a film on the lungs" (76). Eventually, she faints with horror and exhaustion.

Unlike Keitetsi, Mehari is never properly trained to be a soldier; rather she is forced to endure cruel, improvised training sessions organized by Mihret, another girl soldier, only a few years older than she. Mehari hates these sessions and doesn't understand anything she is being told: "She [Mihret] talked about Eritrea, and how we wanted to liberate it . . . I did not understand why Mihret was telling us these things which we had heard thousands of times already" (81). Soon after, during a practice raid, when Mihret tells all of them to "take cover," Mehari has no idea what to do and remains where she is. Older soldiers then beat her so badly that her face bleeds profusely and her shoulder and legs hurt (83). Never fully a soldier, but traumatized by death and destruction, she keeps changing her identity even after she is freed from military service.

Unlike Keitetsi and Mehari, Ishmael Beah, author of *A Long Way Gone,* seems to have had a fairly happy childhood until he was forced into combat. Beah informs us that he grew up in a Muslim family in the village of Mogbwemo, Sierra Leone, West Africa, and that his parents were separated. The narrative focuses primarily on Beah's combat experiences in the Sierra Leonean civil war and his escape and rehabilitation therapy. He wrote the memoir, as he tells us in his acknowledgments, after he had emigrated to the United States and become a college student, with ample help from mentors and friends. However, both specific incidents in the memoir, as well as Beah's sudden elevation to celebrity-like status, provoked a significant controversy. His narrative, moreover, has the potential to cause what Myriam Denov describes as "collective shock, fear, revulsion, intrigue, pride, horror and sympathy" (1) on the part of its Western readers.

Beah began writing his memoir after he enrolled in the creative writing program at Oberlin College in Ohio. His creative writing professor, Dan Chaon, indicated in an interview that Beah told him he wanted to write down his experiences just for his own satisfaction, not for publishing purposes. Soon after, the two of them started meeting once a week, during which time Chaon edited Beah's manuscript. Chaon indicates that he was surprised by Beah's writing abilities, particularly his sentence structure, choice of metaphor, and use of vivid memories (Nason and Gare 6). At the end of two years, Beah and Chaon ended up with a 400-page first draft. When Beah decided to publish the draft with Farrar, Straus and Giroux, the 400 pages were reduced to 229 by Farrar's Sarah Crichton. With regard to any potential errors in the first draft, Chaon's opinion was that they were a result of "poetic license" rather than inaccurate testimony (1). One reviewer of the memoir indicated that regardless of whether the memoir was accurate or not, we as readers should "accept these stories on their own terms or not at all" (Wood 53). Poetic license can, of course, be interpreted in multiple ways. Equiano's famous narrative, mentioned earlier in this chapter, also contained inaccuracies and embellishments, partly because it was written when the eighteenth-century British debate on the slave trade occupied the European public arena. As George Boulukos puts it, knowledge of the details of this debate could help explain why Equiano repeatedly expresses a desire for an "English" identity, and sheds light on why he presented pre-European slavery within Africa in a positive light (247). Likewise, Beah's twentieth-century narrative was partly shaped by twentieth-century media stereotypes about West Africa.

The most important inaccuracy within *A Long Way Gone* has to do with the duration of Beah's time as a child combatant. Early in the narrative, the narrator describes the event that forced Beah to run away from home and become a soldier, namely, the raid, by rebel soldiers, on the villages of Mogbwemo (his home village) and Mattru Jong (where he had gone to participate in a talent show). Beah claims that happened in 1993: "The first time that I was touched by war I was twelve. It was in January of 1993" (6). Toward the middle of the memoir he describes another life-changing event that takes place "in the last weeks of January 1996. I was fifteen" (127). This event, he reveals, is his departure for a UN rehabilitation camp (128–129). These two dates suggest that Beah was a child combatant for three years (1993 to 1996). However, interviews with residents of Mogbwemo conducted by Australian journalists indicate that the attack on Mogbwemo and Mattru Jong occurred in January 1995, not in January 1993; and that between the years 1993 and 1994 Beah was attending the local school, not roaming the country as a child combatant

(Nason and Gare 6). If these facts are true, then, the journalists claim, Beah was a child soldier at age fifteen, not thirteen, and he remained one for three months, not three years (6). Therefore, he could not have participated in many of the events described in the memoir.

Despite the doubts cast on its veracity, Beah's personal saga of violence and escape in *A Long Way Gone* was viewed by some Western journalists as a "heroic transformation from violence to redemption . . . Beah and his constructed transformation from unknown African child soldier to global hero and fashion model is not entirely unique" (Denov 10). In fact, *A Long Way Gone* sold 650,000 hardcover copies in the first year (Nason and Gare 1); it was at number two on the 2007 *New York Times* bestseller list; and *Time* listed it as number three on its top ten list of nonfiction books of 2007. It was praised by authors William Boyd and Sebastian Junger, TV host Jon Stewart lauded it, and even Starbucks sponsored readings and then donated money to UNICEF (Gare 15). After it became a best-seller, Beah started a continuous public-speaking circuit on the topic of child soldiers while also working for Human Rights Watch and UNICEF. His book sales generated enough money for him to live comfortably, first in Brooklyn, New York (Gare 15), and later in Los Angeles, California.[1]

Many early scenes describe, using vivid imagery, the physical and psychological abuse that Beah, along with other recruits to the Sierra Leone Armed Forces, endured during the war. In one scene, Beah is forced to create a new sense of identity by focusing on revenge: "Over and over again in our training he [the training officer] would say that same sentence: Visualize the enemy, the rebels who killed your parents, your family, and those who are responsible for everything that has happened to you" (112). Analyzing this episode, Sanders remarks that "whether these were in fact the corporal's exact words is less important than the fact that, in Beah's recollection, this is what was said" (214). On the same note, Sanders reads the whole memoir as a kind of fantasized wish-fulfillment on Beah's part, suggesting that the murderous revenge and rage that he experienced as a combatant were due to his unconscious "parricidal and fratricidal phantasies," including guilt, punishment, and sibling rivalry (215). Moreover, *A Long Way Gone* appeared two years after Uzodinma Iweala's child soldier novel *Beasts of No Nation,* and Beah may have been influenced by the attention paid to that novel and to the considerable media coverage of the civil wars in Sierra Leone, Liberia, and Côte d'Ivoire. Regardless of whether we read scenes like these as a product of fantasy or media stereotypes, the descriptions themselves suggest that Beah's emotions were volatile. Later in the memoir, the narrative describes an ambush that Beah experiences, in a forest outside his village, when his unit is attacked by Revolutionary United Front rebels. His friends die all around him, and he describes his reaction. He: "raised my gun and pulled the trigger, and I killed a man. Suddenly, as if someone was shooting them inside my brain, all the massacres I had seen since the day I was touched by war began flashing in my head . . . I shot everything that moved, until we were ordered to retreat" (119). This shooting spree leaves him psychologically scarred, and he is unable to eat or sleep for weeks afterward. Later, in the UN rehabilitation camp, he hides his "bayonet inside my pants and a grenade in my pocket. When one of the soldiers came to search me, I pushed him and told him that if he touched me I would kill him" (129). At the end, it is with great difficulty that he is able to integrate into Sierra Leonean society.

In a later scene, Beah befriends one of the nurses at the UN camp. There, after several misadventures, he tries hard to think of the family he was once part of, but is plagued by migraines and nightmares:

I tried to think of my childhood days, but it was impossible, as I kept getting flashbacks of the first time I slit a man's throat. The scene kept surfacing in my memory light lightning on a dark rainy night, and each time it happened, I heard a sharp cry in my head that made my spine hurt . . . I had a severe migraine that night. (Beah 160)

The narrator writes: "I sang for her [his nurse, Esther] the parts of songs I had memorized that day. Memorizing lyrics left me little time to think about what had happened in the war" (163). While the music heals him to some extent, he really finds peace by creating a larger kinship circle. When he is reunited with a long-lost uncle, he does work through his trauma to some extent (178). Eventually, however, it is his work with the UN in New York testifying about his experiences that brings him satisfaction, and his narrative voice changes accordingly. He writes: "I've come to learn that if I am going to take revenge, in that process I will kill another person whose family will want revenge; then revenge and revenge and revenge will never come to an end" (199). This adult voice speaks throughout the narrative, particularly in the later part, suggesting that only when proper reintegration happens will former child soldiers find peace.

Three years after *A Long Way Gone* was published, Beah wrote the foreword to Canadian general and human rights activist Roméo Dallaire's *They Fight Like Soldiers, They Die Like Children.* Part manifesto and part novel, it alternates between appeals to the international community to halt the global use of child soldiers, and fictionalized versions of Dallaire's own violent encounters with child soldiers. As the epigraph at the start of this chapter suggests, those fictionalized accounts reflect Dallaire's actual encounters with war which often ended with the deaths of many children. Significantly, Beah ended his foreword to *They*

Fight Like Soldiers with these words: "I challenge you to read this important and timely work and discover that we as human beings, as nations, as the international community, have the capacity to end the use of children in war. We must not waste another minute as the task is clearly outlined in these pages" (xi). This narrative voice that calls out to the readers to take action is, of course, not evident in the narrative of *A Long Way Gone,* but that narrative does show, as the preceding paragraphs suggest, how important disarmament and rehabilitation are in the process of helping former child soldiers come to terms with their own culpability. That focus on helping them deal with their guilt and pain was also evident in the other two memoirs discussed in this chapter. As Keitetsi pointed out in her interview, "Turning children into soldiers is the biggest crime because children are so vulnerable to abuse and they can't say no." In that same interview, she also suggested that European children are often shocked by her story because they cannot imagine children like themselves not being properly taken care of by adults. They don't understand, she argued, that in the war-torn Uganda of the 1970s, "even if a child had been shot in the leg, she may have had to take care of her wound all by herself." Moreover, leaders of militia groups in Uganda and elsewhere who used and abused child soldiers during their battles with government forces often denied they had done so after they gained access to political power (Keitetsi, interview). Therefore, memoir writers felt obliged to emphasize some details about their combat experiences and omit others. By contrast, Ishmael Beah included the experiences of other child soldiers within his memoir to reinforce his portrayal of war trauma. The extensive investigations of Australian reporters David Nason and Shelley Gare suggest, for example, that Beah could not have personally experienced all the war trauma that he wrote about in *A Long Way Gone,* and that he could not have encountered events in the order in which he described them. Therefore, the possibility remains that Beah incorporated (without attribution) the experiences of some of Sierra Leone's locally well-known child soldiers, such as Alhaji Babah Sawaneh or Kabba Williams, who have not yet chronicled their experiences. Since Sawaneh and Williams are fully aware of the impact that Beah's text has had in North America, they are actively looking for opportunities to make their own stories known.[2] Circumstances like these complicate the narrative structures of the memoirs analyzed in this book, making them ambiguous and contradictory.

These contradictions within the narratives of *Child Soldier, Heart of Fire,* and *A Long Way Gone* also point to the fact that for many African child soldiers, "the 'normal' experience is one of oppression, deprivation, and upheaval; freedom, affluence, and stability—the Western standard of normality—are actually the exception rather than the rule" (Craps, "Beyond Eurocentrism" 53). The three memoirs call attention to the fact that such experiences of oppression and deprivation often continue many years after the conflict is over. Describing a nameless former child combatant living in the West who chose not to make his story known, Myriam Denov writes, "He does not want to be known solely and uni-dimensionally as a former child soldier . . . for him, such celebrity comes at a price and with a heavy burden. How can he reconcile having committed horrible wartime atrocities and then . . . ultimately being rewarded . . . with status and celebrity as a result?" (10). All three memoirs reveal how difficult it is to reconcile these contradictory claims within their narratives. The narrative and stylistic ambiguities and inconsistencies I have described reflect how contradictory and fragmented the identities of child soldiers really are. At once perpetrator and victim, former African child soldiers speak with adult insights about their traumatic childhood experiences, and deal with their lingering trauma by constantly shifting their sense of agency. Their narratives appeal to their local and global readership on ethical and emotional levels by calling attention to the larger historical and political forces that surround them.

CHAPTER 3

Combat as Backdrop
in Young Adult Life Writing

Before they reached my house they began shooting. People
scattered everywhere. Roofs went up in flames. . . . The village
was destroyed. I hoped my parents had fled. I ran back into
the bush to hide, afraid that the gunmen might come back and
capture or kill me. I watched them kill our cattle, set the millet
and sorghum fields on fire, destroy all the things that human life
needs to survive.

— Benson Deng, Alephonsion Deng, and Benjamin Ajak,
They Poured Fire on Us From the Sky

As the previous chapter has shown, the African child soldier
memoir was influenced by sociocultural forces at work in
the public arena and often took on a variety of writing styles
and forms. Throughout the world, there was considerable variation
in twentieth- and twenty-first-century life writing involving the
recollection of childhood traumas. In North America and Europe
in the 1980s and 1990s, as Kay Schaffer and Sidonie Smith point
out, global, collective movements for human rights slowly became identified with a kind of writing that involved remembering

trauma. The focus on trauma, in turn, produced life writing that included memories of traumatic events, and the "trauma memoir" eventually became a genre in its own right (19). In Latin America, the recorded testimonies of poor or indigenous people led to the Latin American *testimonio,* which gave collective voice to struggles against massive state violence. In Africa and Asia, the story of a young citizen's search for education and belonging led to what some critics have called the postcolonial bildungsroman, in which the aftereffects of colonialism were explored. Other kinds of trauma memoirs cited by Schaffer and Smith include survivor narratives in which victims of abuse spoke out, and prison narratives in which political dissidents described their experiences of incarceration (28).

In many parts of sub-Saharan Africa, modern life-writing had its roots in the nineteenth century, in what Kgomotso Masemola calls "missionary self-writing," in which the protagonists were converts to Christianity who brought Western notions of education and culture to their people (344–345). After the 1950s, African writers, such as Wole Soyinka with his *Ake,* sought, via life writing, to replace colonial binaries with explorations of the cultural and political problems created by colonialism, thereby creating new forms of consciousness for their fellow Africans (345). Among the various narrative registers upon which African (and particularly South African) life writing expressed itself were the personal, the communal, the nostalgic, the political, and the fictional (351), all of which included topics such as the clash of values (traditional versus modern), movement (migration versus return), and place (belonging versus rootlessness). Resulting forms of narrative subjectivity were neither traditional nor colonial, as in Es'kia Mphahlele's *The Wanderers,* and narrative styles were reflective of what Masemola calls the tension between "unbelonging and becoming" (346). Unlike Western notions of narrative fragmentation, unbelonging in the African life-writing context meant multiple narrative positions within very specific political contexts, and styles in which writing became a "weapon against oppression" (346).

Narrative fragmentation and notions of unbelonging characterize a variant of the African trauma memoir, namely, what I am calling the African collaborative child soldier memoir. In 2005, three Sudanese "Lost Boys"[1] named Benson Deng, Alephonsion Deng, and Benjamin Ajak wrote a collaborative memoir entitled *They Poured Fire on Us from the Sky,* an excerpt from which appears as the epigraph to this chapter. Many other memoirs about children confronted by violence followed, such as American missionary Donald H. Dunson's *Child, Victim, Soldier: The Loss of Innocence in Uganda* (2008), about the ordeals of children like seven-year-old Sunday Obote who were kidnapped by the Lord's Resistance Army. This chapter focuses on three collaborative memoirs: *Girl Soldier: A Story of Hope for Northern Uganda's Children* (2007) by Ugandan Grace Akallo and American Faith J. H. McDonnell; *The Bite of the Mango* (2008) by Sierra Leonean–Canadian Mariatu Kamara and Canadian Susan McClelland; and *War Child: A Child Soldier's Story* (the novel and the film, 2009) by South Sudanese Emmanuel Jal and British Megan Lloyd Davies. Reformed child soldiers Akallo and Jal and the victim of child soldiers Kamara, all three of whom now live or spend most of their time in the West, wrote about their experiences with some help from foreign professional writers or journalists. The collaborative nature of these memoirs is not their only distinguishing feature, however. Unlike the three memoirs I analyzed in chapter 2, in *Girl Soldier, The Bite of the Mango,* and *War Child* there are few precise details about their protagonists' encounters with combat or with soldiers. Instead, each narrative focuses on the transformative nature of the protagonist's faith or love of music or links to the wider community. The narratives are also characterized by gaps, binary oppositions, strange contradictions, and repeated images and phrases.

A public sphere, writes Joseph Slaughter, is "a story space that not only enables but also shapes and constrains narrative; moreover, it is not simply a clearinghouse for the publication of personal narrative truth but a kind of story factory in which the norms of public discourse become legible" (143–144). The "story space" of *Girl Soldier* is one that centers on events in Grace Akallo's life, in the year 1996. There are two narrators of *Girl Soldier:* the first, Akallo, describes the horrifying details of her kidnapping and servitude with the Lord's Resistance Army (LRA), while the second, McDonnell, provides a very selective historical context for those events. Using an involved first-person narrative style, Akallo describes her happy childhood from the late 1970s to the early 1980s in a Christian family in the village of Kaberikole in northern Uganda, as well as her interrupted high school education at the exclusive St. Mary's College for girls in Aboké. Rather than describe what happened to her after her high school education was interrupted, however, Akallo focuses on the year 1996, when she was kidnapped from St. Mary's and dragged off to war.[2] At this point, Akallo provides copious details of the new life she is now forced to live, including hard labor and sexual exploitation by recruits of the LRA, all of which generate intense fear and acute self-loathing. Akallo also describes her dramatic escape, including brief analyses of how she tried to get back to concentrating on her studies, without the benefits of counseling or rehabilitation. What Akallo omits, however, are several important events following that escape, including her return to Aboké to complete her high school education, her attendance at Uganda Christian University in Mukono, Uganda, and (in 2005) at Gordon College in Wenham, Massachusetts (D. Brown 1). Nor does Akallo provide much information about why she wrote the memoir or why she chose to collaborate with Faith J. H. McDonnell, the director of the conservative Institute on Religion and Democracy's Religious Liberty Program and Church Alliance for a New Sudan. Akallo does provide some brief insights about the writing process in the acknowledgments section of *Girl Soldier*. Here Akallo indicates that she got the idea of writing the memoir from McDonnell (McDonnell and Akallo 17), and McDonnell is, in fact, often listed as its sole author. For example, she is listed as such on the website of the Institute on Religion and Democracy, whose Religious Liberty Program she directs. On its website, the institute describes itself as a "faith-based alliance of Christians who monitor, comment, and report on issues affecting the Church. We seek to reform the Church's role in public life, protect religious freedom, and support democracy at home and abroad" ("Who We Are"). In the acknowledgments section of *Girl Soldier,* McDonnell tells us that Jane Campbell of Chosen Books asked her to write about child soldiers in South Sudan (McDonnell and Akallo 18). Based in Grand Rapids, Michigan, Chosen Books publishes "powerful books that help millions to live the Spirit-filled life . . . [and] help believers to better know and love the Lord Jesus Christ" ("About Chosen Books"). Its goal, the website indicates, is "to publish well-crafted books that recognize the gifts and ministry of the Holy Spirit and help the reader live a more empowered and effective life for Jesus Christ" ("About Chosen Books").

Given the publishing goals of Chosen Books, the narrative thrust of *Girl Soldier* points toward an evangelical rather than a testimonial function. This proselytizing objective is also apparent in the memoir's narrative structure. In eleven odd-numbered chapters, Akallo tells the story of her enslavement and escape; while in eleven even-numbered chapters plus an introduction and a conclusion, McDonnell provides a context for "believers" who "love the Lord Jesus Christ." Not only is this narrative structure somewhat clumsy, but McDonnell dominates the narrative: her sections make up 69 percent of the total pages in the book while Akallo's sections make up 31 percent. More importantly, McDonnell's context, while ostensibly a history of nineteenth- and twentieth-century political violence in Uganda, is, upon closer analysis, extremely depoliticized. Alexandra Schultheis's description of the recent film about Uganda, *Invisible Children: Final Cut* (which McDonnell effusively praises in chapter 22), could be applied to the narrative of *Girl Soldier* too, namely, that it "divorces the crisis in Northern Uganda from the realm of material politics . . . [it depends on] a depoliticized, ultimately self-gratifying depiction of the children . . . [using] a discourse of universalized childhood" (Schultheis 35). McDonnell uses a discourse of universalized evangelical zeal to describe the rapid spread of Christianity in 1870s Uganda, for example, indicating that it "threatened powerful witch doctors and Arab Muslims who operated the slave trade and promoted Islam" (McDonnell and Akallo 41). Not only does McDonnell use exaggerated binaries like this one, setting off "good" Christian missionaries against "ignorant" African witch doctors, and "evil" Arab slave traders, but she also completely omits any analysis of the structures of power that fueled both Western missionary activities and the ideology of Joseph Kony. Summarizing the factors that led to Kony's rise, for example, McDonnell suggests that it resulted from the "struggle between Christianity, Islam and spiritism that is still going on" (37). Later in the narrative, McDonnell presents divine mediation as the preferred solution to the problem of Joseph Kony. She writes: "God's intervention to save the children of northern Uganda is evident today in many ways and many circumstances. Sometimes the circumstances were miraculous, as they were with Grace Akallo" (196). Toward the end of the narrative, therefore, McDonnell calls on her readers to use the "power of prayer" (216) to help the children of Uganda.

Like McDonnell, Akallo also evokes the "power of prayer" repeatedly in the narrative, and uses unusual images to describe her physical abuse and sexual exploitation. Writing about the effects of multiple and repeated exposure to interpersonal violence, physician Laura S. Brown suggests that it produces "complex trauma" (4). Akallo uses animal metaphors to describe this complex trauma, equating her treatment by the LRA to that of a work animal being seasoned. In one scene, for example, Akallo describes how she is made to watch as LRA soldiers kill a girl who had tried to escape, by smashing her head to pieces (McDonnell and Akallo 106). Like Senait Mehari and Mariatu Kamara, Akallo never actually kills civilians, but is forced to wander through the countryside surrounding the Gulu and Kitgum districts, raiding villages and abducting children (107). In another scene, Akallo describes how she was punished by LRA commander B. M. Oyet, because she had lost a tent and had mislaid a cooking pot while camped in the woods. She writes: "Everybody who lived under this man was called to witness the [i.e., Akallo's] killing. That is what they usually do when they are killing someone . . . I reached where he was seated, and everyone looked on like I was a goat taken for slaughter for Christmas" (108). Fortunately, Oyet is "not in the mood to kill" (108), but that does little to dissipate Akallo's sense that she is a beast ready to be slaughtered.

Akallo repeats this strategy of comparing her captivity and abuse to that of a work animal in many other scenes. After meeting Joseph Kony himself in South Sudan, Akallo and the other girls spend most of their waking hours scrounging for food, much like animals working in a pack. Akallo writes, "We were forced to eat lizards, rats, wild fruits, leaves, roots and soil" (110). In another scene, Akallo provides graphic details about her rape by Lakati, an LRA commander older than her own father.[3] She writes: "He seized me and forced me to bed. I felt like a thorn was in my skin as my innocence was destroyed" (110). In the movie, *Grace, Milly, Lucy* (analyzed later in this chapter) Akallo, speaking via a voice-over, describes her rapes by Lakati as "affecting her spirit forever," after which she reads out this passage about thorns. Clinicians like Laura Brown have indicated that people suffering from PTSD as a result of repeated sexual abuse often experience a sense of debilitating pain, so Grace's description of Akallo's believing she is being pierced by thorns is accurate (L. Brown 110). In later scenes in the memoir, Akallo describes three suicide attempts, which, she tells us, were prevented only by the timely intervention of other kidnapped girls (McDonnell and Akallo 114). Eventually, Akallo, like Kamara, turns within, as she hears a voice inside her head urging her to escape.

Before describing her escape, Akallo provides some details about her attempts to convince herself that her life is worth living. She writes: "I lived for a long time only in hopelessness. I assumed I would die of starvation or thirst. Or I would be beaten to death with sticks and pangas, or machetes . . . I despaired when he [her friend Paul] died, because I did not die. I did not understand why" (McDonnell and Akallo 125). She is motivated to stay alive only by her faith in God and her dreams of peace. When she sleeps, she dreams of escape routes, involving perilous river crossings, in which she swims to freedom while her companions drown (126). Once awake, she does run away, along with other girls, and ends up near the shores of a tributary of the Blue Nile. She wades across it and eventually meets up with soldiers from the Sudan People's Liberation Army, who take her back to Uganda and freedom. Her dreams of freedom evidently fuel her attempts to escape.

Akallo provides some details about her life after she escapes. She mentions that her dominant emotions are helplessness and guilt because she escaped but her friends did not (190). Akallo does not provide much information about how she dealt with this guilt and trauma. In an interview Akallo gave after the memoir was published, she confessed:

> Talking has never killed anybody. My friends who remain in captivity cannot talk. If they could, they would scream. They would cry. But they cannot. I have a chance. . . . If God had not taken me to see what was happening, I would not be speaking about it. Maybe I would just be saying, "I can't do anything." But that is not what I say. (Blunt 39)

Here, Akallo presents her ability to talk and write as emanating from her captivity and not the other way around, possibly in an effort to prove that her captivity had not turned her into a silent victim. The memoir ends, however, with Akallo's call to action, an imperative that is also quoted in the movie *Grace, Milly, Lucy:* "To the whole world, this is my cry: There is no future without healthy children who grow up in a peaceful environment. Do not turn your hatred on the children" (McDonnell and Akallo 195). The movie, rather than the memoir, shows how Akallo heeded her own calls to action, providing details of her activities with other survivors to "raise awareness" and counsel and provide support to other survivors.

Besides the unusual structure of the narrative, *Girl Soldier* is different from the memoirs in chapter 2 in other ways, too. Unlike Keitetsi, Mehari, and Beah, Akallo became a public figure before, and not as a result of, the writing of her memoir. In fact, her public appearances may have led McDonnell to approach her about writing the book in the first place. Many important details about her kidnapping surfaced only in interviews she did after the memoir was published. In one interview, for example, she explained that she was kidnapped and brutalized by the LRA for seven months (Duin 6) and that after she escaped, she returned to St. Mary's and got her high school certificate. In a movie made about her, she indicates simply that she was driven by her strong desire for an education. In other interviews, she reveals that while in high school, she began working as a counselor in a center for escaped child combatants (D. Brown 1). In 2002, she attended Uganda Christian University in Mukono, Uganda. While there, she got a visa to travel to New York to visit Amnesty International. In New York, she met students who had gone on an exchange program from Gordon College, a Christian college near Boston, in Wenham, Massachusetts. She applied for a scholarship from there and received it in 2005, when she left Uganda Christian and moved to the United States to study at Gordon (1). She majored in communications (Duin 6). In April 2006, the year before the memoir was published, she testified on Capitol Hill about the conflict in Uganda and became, in the words of a *Washington Times* reporter, a "poster child for Congress' efforts to pressure Uganda to end what's been called one the world's worst humanitarian crises" (6). In May 2006, she testified about her experiences before the House Subcommittee on Africa, Global Human Rights and International Operations. In 2007, the year she wrote the memoir, she graduated with a BA from Gordon (6). She eventually went on to get a master's degree. Although all of these important events had taken place before the memoir was written, none of them appear in the narrative.

Three years after *Girl Soldier* was written, Akallo's story reappeared in another format. She appeared in a fifty-two-minute documentary movie entitled *Faith, Grace, Lucy, Child Soldiers* (2010), directed by Raymonde Provencher, produced by the National Film Board of Canada, and distributed by Women Make Movies and Amazon Video. The documentary tells the story of Akallo and two other girls who had also escaped from captivity by the LRA: Milly Auma and Lucy Lanyero. The movie starts and ends with a quote from *Girl Soldier:* "To the whole world this is my cry . . . do not turn your hatred on the children" (Provencher). Some of the movie's early scenes provide details (narrated by each girl in turn) about how they were abducted and what they did after they escaped. In this regard, the movie includes more information about the combat experience than the memoir does. We learn, for example, that Auma and Lanyero were enslaved for ten years each and that, therefore, their trauma was more debilitating than Akallo's was. Since Auma and Lanyero had only a rudimentary education with no access to employment outside their village, they rely, after their escapes, on local healers and extended families for counseling and support.[4] By contrast, Akallo is shown talking to reporters and giving speeches in the UN General Assembly (often sitting alongside Ishmael Beah), raising public awareness. In one scene, Akallo confesses that the main reason she keeps talking about her experiences is because she wants someone to rescue her still-captive friends. Significantly, Akallo is the only speaker in the movie who narrates her story in English; both Auma and Lanyero speak in Acholi. Later scenes in the movie reveal how Auma and Lanyero founded an organization named Empowering Hands to help children affected by war. Although many other girls who were kidnapped by the LRA also appear in the movie, they speak much less than Akallo, Auma, and Lanyero. As Akallo says near the end of the movie, "Girls don't talk much."

Five years after *Faith, Grace, Lucy, Child Soldiers* was released, a young-adult version of Akallo's story was published. Entitled *Out in Front: Grace Akallo and the Pursuit of Justice for Child Soldiers* (2015), it was written by Kem Knapp Sawyer in a narrative style suitable for a preteen readership, full of glossy pictures of the school, the rebels, and the nuns. With evocative chapter titles like "The Den of Death" or "Get Up and Go," it features three-paragraph summaries inserted between the story of Akallo's abduction, on such topics as the colonial history of Uganda or American boy soldiers during the American Civil War. Sawyer relies on stereotypes and overgeneralized descriptors for important places and people. He turns Kony, for example, into "an internationally sought-after former Catholic choir boy turned warlord" (8), while describing northern Uganda and southern Sudan as places filled with "swirling brown rivers that coil like intestines and are infested with crocodiles" (21). *Girl Soldier,* the memoir, is mentioned on page 51 and is described as a critically acclaimed autobiography. The exaggerations and inaccuracies in this young adult version of Akallo's story notwithstanding, its very existence suggests that its content remains appealing to a variety of demographics in North America and Europe. This appeal seems to have less to do with the specifics of Akallo's encounter with the LRA than with stereotypes prevalent in the West about encounters between children and rebels in Uganda.

Encountering rebels is not something that eleven-year-old Mariatu Kamara would have imagined doing. Kamara's background is similar to Beah's: she grew up in a Muslim household in rural Sierra Leone and was profoundly affected by its civil war. Unlike Beah, however, she was not a soldier but a victim, and in this regard, her story links more to Akallo's than to Beah's. Three years after Akallo was dragged off by LRA rebels in northern Uganda, Kamara's village in Sierra Leone was overrun by the RUF rebels, who mutilated her body, traumatizing her to such an extent that she tried, on multiple occasions, to kill herself. *The Bite of the Mango* uses a first-person, involved narrative style to describe Kamara's excruciating encounter with the rebels, focusing on how it changed the course of her life. Although Kamara was never recruited or enslaved by rebel soldiers, she was raped at a young age by a relative. After recovering from the injuries the rebels inflicted on her, she lived in a Freetown slum, begging for a living. Near the end of the memoir the narrator describes how Kamara immigrated to Canada, where, after a period of withdrawal, she completes her high school education. What the memoir does not mention, but that Kamara explained in interviews, is that after graduating from high school she enrolled in college as a family counseling major ("Nigeria"). In other interviews, Kamara claimed that she was encouraged to write the memoir by Beah himself, whom she met while she was visiting New York. She reached out to Canadian journalist Susan McClelland for assistance, and they wrote the memoir together. After the writing was completed, Beah wrote an introduction for her. Before the memoir was published, both McClelland and Kamara traveled to Sierra Leone to fact-check the events and people mentioned in it (Neill).

Unlike Akallo, Kamara became well known after, and not before, she wrote her memoir, when she began to speak publicly for Free the Children and then became UNICEF's Special Representative for Children in Armed Conflicts. As news reports and interviews indicate, soon after the memoir was published, Kamara toured Canada and Sierra Leone and talked to Sierra Leonean president Ernest Bai Koroma about the plight of amputees (Neill). In some interviews, she has indicated that her goal is to work for the UN to raise awareness of the impact of war on children ("Nigeria"). In particular, she claims that she wants to alleviate the abject poverty that characterizes the lives of Sierra Leonean children whose limbs were amputated by rebels, because despite promises of medical and educational help from the Sierra Leonean government, nothing much has been done to help them (Neill).

In *The Bite of the Mango,* Kamara describes her first encounter with the rebels, using images that evoke a nightmare. Kamara is completely confused when the rebels come to her village, Magborou, kidnap her, and force her to watch as they kill those who are near and dear to her. The narrator writes: "The rebel looked no older than I was . . . I started to cry. I had never seen anyone die before, let alone be killed. But the rebel said he would kill me if I didn't stop crying" (Kamara and McClelland 30). Believing, mistakenly, that she is about to be recruited into their army, Kamara pretends obedience. She is rewarded with a question from one of the rebels, a question she doesn't understand. He asks her which hand she prefers to have cut off first. When she is too scared to answer, the teenage rebels pick up her right hand and cut it off, and the narrator describes this horrifying event in graphic detail:

> As the machete came down, things went silent. I closed my eyes tightly but then they popped open and I saw everything. It took the boy two attempts to cut off my right hand. The first swipe didn't get through the bones, which I saw sticking out in all different shapes and sizes. (40–41)

When the boy soldier finally succeeds in severing Kamara's right hand from her arm, the narrator describes, in a strangely impersonal way, her hand's fishlike twitches, indicating that its movements reminded her of the desperate leaps of captured trout "when we caught them from the river, before we knocked them on the head and killed them to cook for our evening meal" (41).

As if that gruesome comparison of her own dismembered hand to a twitching trout isn't bad enough, the narrator goes on to describe the agonizing severing of Kamara's left arm, which takes the boy soldier three tries to complete. At this point, according to the narrator: "some of the flesh remained and hung precariously loose. I didn't feel any pain . . . But my legs gave way" (41). Soon after, Kamara passes out and later, makes a slow and painful hitchhiking trip across the countryside to Freetown, where she is treated in government hospitals. At the end of her ordeal, her arms slowly heal, but the hospital doctors inform her that she is pregnant. The narrator describes Kamara's confusion upon hearing this, and there is a flashback to an incident that has hitherto been omitted from the narrative. The flashback centers around a repressed memory that now surfaces in Kamara's consciousness involving a sexual assault she had endured, perpetrated by an elderly acquaintance, about which she had remained silent. The narrative returns to the present, with descriptions of several attempted suicides that the traumatized Kamara inflicts upon herself, having run away from the hospital. The narrator describes how her newly-made friends in the Freetown slum she lives in intervene, not only saving her life, but providing her with much-needed support and a sense of community. This narrative (trauma, healing, purposelessness) underscores how Kamara's trauma, rather than originating in a single event (the encounter with rebels), is based in many different frightening encounters (the loss of her hands, her earlier rape), making her recovery difficult.

Much of the narrative in the middle section of the memoir focuses on the precariousness of Kamara's mental health. Several scenes describe her severe depression and emotional instability, both of which are complicated by her painful labor and delivery. After Abdul, her baby boy, dies, she chooses extreme confinement, convinced that her inability to love him has caused his death (108–109). She spends much of her time asleep and often has nightmares (109). She is only able to heal after agreeing to perform in a play about AIDS, organized by a friend, after which, the narrator indicates, "Some of the heaviness inside of me had started to lift. Victor [the theater director] was right: pretending to cry onstage did offer some relief from my pain" (115). This activity gives her a sense of purpose, and she finally overcomes her depression and dejection.

The later sections of the memoir describe Kamara's attempts to create a sense of community for herself in Toronto. As trauma

clinician Boris Cyrulnik suggests, the support of a social community is the key factor in helping traumatized children to become resilient, because "the main factors of resilience are the
affect provided by relatives and friends, as well as the meaning
attributed to the fact by the historical and social context" (28).
Social workers connect Kamara with the Toronto-based Sierra
Leonean community, where she makes lasting friendships. The
narrator writes: "When I fell asleep that night, my head was filled
with happy thoughts. I really loved being around Kadi, Abou, and
their family and eating Sierra Leonean food again. My mind was
soon flooded with so many thoughts of home" (Kamara and Mc-
Clelland 171). After several relapses, during which she withdraws
and stops communicating (177–178), causing her new "family" to
rally around her, she continues with her ESL classes and becomes
interested in storytelling. Telling her story to an audience eventually furthers her healing process, and this continues when one
of her high school teachers introduces her to Ishmael Beah. The
narrator describes Kamara's meeting with Beah in detail, ending
with her question to him: "Do you think anyone will want to read
a book about me?" (199) and his response: "Yes . . . yes" (199).
The memoir ends at this point, suggesting that the ability to tell
her story will, in the future, heal her complex trauma. This sug-
gestion is supported by Kamara's activities after the memoir was
published. In her various public appearances she spoke not just
about her own traumatic experiences, but also about her cultural
heritage. As she said in an interview with Susan McClelland, "It is
important for Sierra Leonean stories to be heard. The country has
a rich history. . . . Once Sierra Leoneans take pride in reading the
stories of others, some may become confident to write about our
own culture, to let the world know who we are, so we can have a
sense of a pride in ourselves" (McClelland). This focus on taking
pride in her own heritage suggests that for Kamara, writing and

speaking about her recovery from a traumatic experience war has a profound testimonial value. In *The Bite of the Mango,* the details of the war and its attendant atrocities are, narratively speaking, less important than the process of overcoming them.

Unlike Kamara, Emmanuel Jal, the protagonist of *War Child,* spent a good part of his teenaged years fighting and killing. In the early part of *War Child,* Jal tells us that his father, Simon, is a clandestine official in the Sudanese People's Liberation Army (SPLA), and a member of the Nuer tribe, while his mother, Angelina, is half-Nuer, half-Dinka, and a practicing Christian. The narrative unfolds in chronological order, its early chapters focusing on the first seven years of Jal's life, when his village, in present-day South Sudan, was peaceful. Then the narrative shifts to the year 1987, when, right after Jal turned seven, the war comes to his village and he is sent to a school far away from home. At age eleven (and eight years before Kamara was attacked by rebels in Sierra Leone), Jal becomes a soldier with the SPLA. Jal describes his combat experiences until, at the age of twelve, he joins a group of four hundred boy soldiers who desert the SPLA and trek eastward across Sudan's badlands, mud patches, and minefields, till they reach Waat, in eastern Sudan. In the second half of *War Child,* Jal describes how, in Waat, he meets Emma McCune, a British aid worker working for a Canadian charity that helps rescue child soldiers. McCune takes Jal to Kenya, showers him with love and care, provides him with a house and education, and encourages him to make friends with Kenyan boys. The narrator writes about the devastation Jal felt when, in 1994, McCune is killed in a car accident. He begins living in Nairobi's slums, helped only by Emma's close circle of friends and a small income he generates from creating rap music. In successive chapters, the narrator focuses on how Jal manages to graduate from high school despite his setbacks, and goes on to the University of Westminster in England to study engineering. However, his education is cut short when his British visa expires and British immigration authorities refuse to renew it. He returns to Kenya, joins a church choir, and begins doing rap performances.

In 2009, a year after Jal had already released a music album entitled *Warchild* (which I analyze later in this chapter), Jal undertook the process of writing his story down as a memoir. He cowrote it with British journalist Megan Lloyd Davies. Davies (a former *Daily Mirror* reporter) indicated that the writing experience with Jal was difficult because "Emmanuel had never told his whole life story before. Over months of interviews, he slowly got to know and trust me enough tell it" ("Megan Lloyd Davies"). In the early chapters of *War Child,* Jal uses vivid language to describe the acute trauma he experienced as a young child soldier. He writes: "With the smell of burning flesh in the air and the memories of bodies lying still on the ground, I'd run as if the devil were chasing me. I became good at war" (Jal and Davies 28). The narrator also describes the grueling indoctrination process Jal underwent, including heavy beatings and imprisonments and emotional brainwashing. Jal uses vivid images to describe how SPLA officers taught him to hate the Arabic-speaking northern Sudanese militiamen, whom they called Arabs, or *jallabas:* "The Arabs . . . are to blame for every drop of blood spilled. . . . They have destroyed our people, our homes, our land, and our religion" (73). These words had a deep impact on Jal: "Anger pricked hot and sharp inside me. I felt the bitter taste of hate slide down the back of my throat and burn its way to the tips of my toes. The spear settled in my chest once more" (74). This description of the corrosive nature of ethnic hatred echoes the findings of clinicians like Boris Cyrulnik, who describes hatred as a "cohesive factor that precludes forgiveness and resilience" (27). In *War Child,* Jal uses hyperbole to explain how a combination of hatred, anger, and guilt turned him into a merciless fighter. In one scene, he describes how, after he killed three *jallabas* in a shoot-out, he felt exhilaration, confusion, and revulsion:

> The bodies were blank, lifeless, just as I'd always dreamed they would be. The sound of the battle beat inside my chest as I stared down. The faces of the dead swam in front of me as I looked at them.
>
> My eyes focused for a second. I felt breathless.
>
> These were not Arab faces. They were black like mine. My stomach turned. Where were the *jallabas?* (Jal and Davies 141)

Jal's commanding officer compounds his confusion by admitting that although two-thirds of the northern Sudanese army comprised "black Muslims," they were "worse than Arabs" because they had betrayed "their own people, and for that they deserve to die like dogs" (141). In another scene, the narrator focuses on Jal's encounter with a wounded, prostrated northern Sudanese soldier in a way that suggests that Jal has taken his commanding officer's rhetoric to heart. He writes: "I lifted my machete as the other boys raised theirs and smashed them into the *jallaba*. Blood spit warm onto my face. . . . I hit the man twice more. . . . He wouldn't die" (157).

Later chapters in the narrative focus on the ways in which surrogate mothers and music help Jal come to terms with this confusion and revulsion. This process also involves dealing with feelings of guilt, and it occurs after he has become one of the four hundred "Lost Boys" who made the long trek across Sudan (only sixteen of the four hundred survived) (Boustany M06). As one critic argued, Jal's healing process is a result of "the grace of two women who steer him toward education. His subsequent life as a rapper and philanthropist trying to save other children from similar pain and

anguish leaves hope for the possibility of redemption" (Romero).
Many scenes in the memoir indicate that Jal's surrogate mother,
Emma McCune, had a profound impact on him. The narrator
writes: "Emma [McCune] never laughed or shouted back at me .
. . and so I took without thinking what Emma, and other people
around her, gave because I had forgotten what love was" (Jal and
Davies 181). In the song "War Child" on the CD *Warchild,* Jal describes how he felt when McCune died: "The pain I carry / Is too
much to handle / Who's there please to light my candle / Is there
anyone to hear my cry / Here I am pale and dry." The memoir
describes how Jal formed his own music band in Kenya and made
a name and an income for himself first with gospel and soul music
and, later, as a rapper. While the music gave him both a creative
outlet and an economic boost, it also helped him reunite with lost
family members. In one scene, Jal describes his chance meeting
with Nyaruach, his long-lost and traumatized sister. He writes:
"As I looked into my sister's [shadowed and sad] eyes, I felt more
and more that this [his country and war] was something I wanted
to write about. I had learned to stop hating *jallabas* in the years
since I started learning to forgive" (Jal and Davies 232–233). Details
about Nyaruach's sadness are provided in the song "Vagina" on
Warchild: "My children are hungry / And my back in pain / And
yet they come to rape again." Many chapters in the memoir show
how, despite the atrocities inflicted upon his family members, Jal's
songwriting enables him to give up his deep feelings of hatred.
After Jal is called on to testify about the atrocities at the UN, he
learned "to transform the hate burning inside this boy [Jal's former
self] into love . . . to leave him behind . . . to forget the message the
war child had taught me" (Jal and Davies 246).

Despite *War Child*'s graphic details about Jal's combat experience, several episodes are left incomplete. For example, the narrative leaves unfinished the full extent that wartime brainwashing

had on Jal. In interviews Jal gave after the memoir was published, however, he mentions that "most of Sudan's lost boys were bitter and wanted revenge. Just a bit of an ignition could set us off. You are hate-driven. I was hate-driven" (Boustany M06). These interviews also explain why the later chapters in the memoir focus so much on Jal's activities as a musician. In an interview, Jal pointed out that "music is powerful. It is the only thing that can speak into your mind, your heart and your soul without your permission . . . music helped me as a person, and it creates awareness about my people" (Batey 28). This comment by Jal underscores the close connections he made between healing and music. These connections are given somewhat short shrift in *War Child.* One of the events Jal mentions briefly in his narrative is the fact that in 2005, the SPLA (now renamed SPLM, or Sudanese People's Liberation Movement) came to power in the new country of South Sudan. By this time, as journalists following his career have shown, Jal had released his first album, *Gua,* in which he had rapped about war in Arabic, English, Nuer, and Dinka (Batey 28). In 2008, he released two albums. The first was *Ceasefire,* with celebrated Sudanese musician Abdel Gadir Salim, as an "exercise in Christian-Muslim collaboration" (Denselow 14). The second was *Warchild,* which told his life story as a child soldier in a combination of commercial pop and hip-hop. With lyrics in English, he tells us in the song "Forced to Sin," "I lived with an AK-47 / By my side / Slept with one eye open wide / Run / Duck / Play dead / Hide / I've seen my people die like flies." In the title song, "War Child," he says: "I believe I've survived for a reason, to tell my story, to touch lives." One reviewer found the album more "interesting for his story and his message" than for his music, because the biblical references, gospel influences, dancehall reggae, and African chanting created an odd mixture of effects (Denselow 14). Another reviewer liked the narrative, describing it as flowing "between darkness

and light, the terror that befell his family and kinsmen, the horrors he went on to inflict upon others, and a deep-seated desire
to set things right" (Boustany M06). Some of the songs from his
original album eventually became the soundtrack for the movie
Blood Diamond and the TV series *ER* (Boustany M06). Later in
2008, *Warchild* became the basis of a documentary movie called
War Child. Produced by Interface Media and the Global Fund for
Children, it is about Jal's life. It mentions some incidents omitted
from his memoir, such as the fact that he found out that Nyakouth,
his older sister, had become a sex slave to a warlord who sexually
and physically abused her. It also mentions other details about
healing, such as the fact that Jal was eventually reunited with his
other sister, Nyaruach (mentioned earlier in this chapter), who,
after being repeatedly raped and traumatized, heard Jal singing on
BBC and snuck her way into Kenya to meet him (Boustany M06).
Given the duration of Jal's career as a musician, it was his music
rather than his memoir that enabled him to tell his story fully.
However, even his album had its limitations. As early as 2008,
Jal had a falling out with his music producer, Peter Moszynski,
who had helped him tremendously after McCune had died. In
order to get out of his record contract with Moszynski, Jal hired
lawyers who accused Moszynski of exploiting and enslaving Jal.
This incident left Moszynski angry and bitter (Boustany M06).
Overall, both the album and the memoir focus less on the details
of Jal's combat experience than on his use of music to heal. The
combat experience, while narrated graphically, ultimately becomes the backdrop for Jal's ability to use music to heal himself
from the trauma of war.

   In all three memoirs discussed in this chapter, the writing
process complicates the issue of narrative uncertainty. Although
the entire narrative of *War Child* may not have been written
down before Jal became a musician, by the time the memoir was

published he had made a name for himself as a rapper. Therefore, particularly in the scenes during which Jal describes his activities as a musician, narrative chronology becomes less important than how he used music to put his life back together. *Girl Soldier,* for all its focus on the abuse of Ugandan girls in combat, is really an inspirational tale for Christian evangelists rather than a story about combat trauma. The details of Akallo's combat experience are the means to rally support for McDonnell's "praying for peace" effort, and historical and factual accuracy are jettisoned. The narrative of *The Bite of the Mango* emphasizes Kamara's will to survive and her strong ties within her community. The pain and suffering she experiences during her ordeal, while described vividly, are not the point of her narrative. The collaborative "I"s that speak to us in all three narratives draw attention to the difficulties of constructing coherent narratives about war by writers who either have limited language skills or little firsthand exposure to war. For Akallo, writing about wartime sexual exploitation required personal faith, inner courage, and the ability to reach out to North American audiences. As she indicated in a short article she wrote as a college student in the United States: "After 17 years of war, we [Ugandans] want our lives back. . . . The time has come. We must stop this war" (Akallo). Kamara's ability to overcome her physical and emotional brutalization at the hands of the RUF was dependent on the support she eventually got from the global Sierra Leonean community. As she said in a 2014 interview, "God took away my hands so I can touch the world with my heart" (Caton). Jal healed himself from his combat trauma only when he had access to an international entertainment infrastructure. Complicating these healing processes further is the flexible format of all three texts. The storylines of *Girl Soldier* and *War Child* (and to a lesser extent *The Bite of the Mango*) appeared in multimedia formats (films, tapes, social media), thereby appealing to multiple audiences. These collaborative recollections of war, with their multiple narrators and diverse formats, simultaneously connect the narratives to multiple audiences. They also highlight all the narrative ambiguities and discontinuities within the African child soldier memoir as a whole.

CHAPTER 4

Narrative Uncertainty in Child Soldier Fiction

> About suffering they were never wrong,
> The Old Masters: how well they understood
> Its human position; how it takes place
> While someone else is eating or opening a
> window or just walking dully along.
>
> —W. H. Auden, "Musée des Beaux Arts"

U nlike the "Old Masters" in the epigraph, the narrative voice in *Sozaboy,* a novel about a child's experience of war, is that of Mene, an uneducated Nigerian adolescent, who understands the realities of war only after he has lost everything. A voice created by the late Nigerian novelist and activist Ken Saro-Wiwa, it tells the story of the Nigerian civil war in an intensely subjective way, making no attempt to maintain factual accuracy about the battles and conflicts Mene gets caught up in. Soon after the turn of the twentieth century, Ivoirian novelist Ahmadou Kourouma, as well as Congolese-American novelist Emmanuel Dongala and Nigerian-American novelist Uzodinma Iweala, all produced novels about African children experiencing war. Like Saro-Wiwa,

Kourouma, Dongala, and Iweala are civilians with no combat experience; nevertheless, the episodes within Kourouma's *Allah Is Not Obliged* (2006, translated from *Allah n'est pas obligé,* 2000), Dongala's *Johnny Mad Dog* (2005, translated from *Johnny Chien Méchant,* 2002), and Iweala's *Beasts of No Nation* (2005) were based closely on the experiences of real-life African children at war. Like *Sozaboy,* these three novels are highly subjective accounts of war, but unlike *Sozaboy,* they are characterized by narrative uncertainty. They present combat as absurd and ambiguous. Moreover, they do not utilize the kinds of narrative motifs that critics have associated with the African war novel, namely, the "song of my country," the "male warrior as war personified," the "ordeal in the forest," and the "landscape of eternity" (Coundouriotis, *People's Right* 26). Eleni Coundouriotis defines the "song of my country" as a trope in which the tortured African body becomes the site of war, its suffering enacting a form of resistance (26). In the "male warrior as war personified," ordinary African identity within a particular community is transformed by violence (26). In the "ordeal in the forest," a journey into the African wilderness becomes transformative and the protagonist takes steps to determine the outcome of the war (27–28). In "landscape of eternity," the imagined pristine African landscape heals or transcends the destructive effects of war (28). All four together, Coundouriotis argues, can have the effect of creating an allegory of "resistance and aspiration, the outside of war" (24).

Unlike the protagonists of the African war novel, the central characters within the African child soldier novel have ambiguous and unfulfilled motivations. As Coundouriotis has argued elsewhere, when real-life child soldiers committed criminal acts, these were sometimes attributed to abuse or drug addiction, enabling the child to move "seamlessly from perpetrator to victim" ("Arrested Historicization" 192–194).[1] Birahima, Johnny, and Agu, the three child soldiers at the centers of *Allah Is Not Obliged, Johnny Mad Dog,* and *Beasts of No Nation,* are uncertain protagonists. On the one hand, they participate, directly or indirectly, in cruel and outlandish crimes; on the other hand, they abruptly cease their violent acts for ambiguous reasons. Both perpetrator and victim, they negotiate a liminal space somewhere between perpetrator at one moment and victim the next. Acutely attentive to their global audiences, they are profoundly displaced from their local communities. In this chapter, I will show how the form of these three novels, like their protagonists, are ambivalent: the involved first-person narration is reminiscent of the memoirs described in the previous two chapters, while images and scenes replicate each other to the point of absurdity. The only certitudes these novels present about war are confusion and horror.

Allah Is Not Obliged unfolds, as do *A Long Way Gone* and *A Bite of the Mango,* during the Sierra Leonean civil war that included Liberia and Côte d'Ivoire. *Johnny Mad Dog* takes place during the three-year civil war in the Republic of Congo, while *Beasts of No Nation* describes a fictional country resembling Nigeria during its civil war in the 1960s. Writing about recent trends within African Francophone literature, Odile Cazenave points out that since the 1980s, fictional depictions of violence have become much more graphic (59), with children and youth becoming agents rather than objects of violence (60).[2] Birahima, Johnny, and Agu remain outside their communities at the end; the narratives leave their rehabilitation and "normalization" process unfinished (62).

This representation, within these three novels, of former child soldiers as outsiders is reflective of present-day realities in West Africa. Even young West Africans who were untouched by war were often, at the turn of the twentieth century, called upon to perform, on behalf of their nations, complex social and cultural responsibilities (Diouf, "Engaging" 4). Therefore, they were deeply affected when nationalist and economic models within their countries failed. As Catherine Bolten has suggested, young West Africans, during times of conflict, become "socialized to violence," and this gives them social leverage and power they have had never had before. In postconflict periods, they identify as victims and gravitate to foreign, rather than domestic, reconciliation models, alienating themselves further in the process. Many ex-combatants end up with no clearly defined social positions within their societies (Bolten 498). *Allah Is Not Obliged* reflects all these ambiguities with regard to the social position of former child soldiers. Its narrative is also uncertain on several levels. The first-person narrator, Birahima, despite drawing attention to his youth (he is a ten-year-old Ivoirian child), speaks with the authority of an adult expert, knowledgeable not just about his own wartime experiences, but also about those of other West African children. The narrator has little faith in the efficacy of humanitarian organizations, and, like one of the narrators of *Johnny Mad Dog,* he uses language in profane, violent, and vulgar ways (Coundouriotis, "Arrested Historicization" 194). More a marker of his agency than his victimization (195), this narrator's voice has been described by critics as having a "pervasive sense of cynicism" (Kearney 83). For one thing, he constantly draws attention to his own "sinfulness," telling us at the outset that rather than being an innocent child, he is "cursed because I did bad things to my maman . . . if your mother is angry with you and she dies with all that anger in her heart, then she curses you and you are cursed" (Kourouma 4). Besides his sense of being cursed, he is opportunistic and greedy and rejoices when Yacouba, the con man who was supposed to be taking him across the Ivoirian border to his aunt's house in Liberia, tells him that instead of living with his aunt, he could become a child soldier and get rich quick. The narrator says: "I shouted Walahé! Walahé! I want to go to Liberia. Right now this minute.

I want to be a child-soldier, a small-soldier" (37). These constant references to the narrator's cynicism remove the possibility of a "perpetrator turned victim" narrative from emerging.

Other events in the novel suggest that explicating Birahima's corruption or cynicism isn't really the point of the narrative. The events the narrator focuses on, after Birahima becomes a soldier, have less to do with combat than with analyses of UN mission failures and the activities of West African warlords like Liberia's Charles Taylor and Sierra Leone's Samuel Doe (Kearney 76). In one scene, the narrator labels Taylor a "barefaced liar, an out-and-out thief, a crook" because he has destroyed Liberia with his racketeering, bribing, and tendency to send child soldiers on "murderous missions" (Kourouma 61). Even as the narrator says this, he grudgingly admires Taylor's ability to play "what people in Africa with its barbaric dictatorships and liberticidal fathers of nations call 'la grande politique.' (According to my Larousse, 'liberticidal' means 'that which destroys freedom.')" (61). This kind of about-face is typical in the narrative, underscored by the narrator's constant ironic references to dictionary definitions of commonly used words and phrases. Although Jack Kearney regards the narrator's attention to historical detail a drawback in the novel (76), I would argue that the constant narrative fluctuation between critique and admiration, cynicism and confusion, makes the narrative uncertain.

Other instances of narrative uncertainty abound in the novel. When the narrator first introduces Papa le Bon, the warlord Birahima works for, his description is filled with tedious repetition, trivial details, and cynical asides. He writes:

> Colonel Papa le Bon was wearing a white soutane, a white soutane tied at the waist with a leather belt, a belt held up by a pair of black leather braces crossed across his back and his chest.

Colonel Papa le Bon was wearing a cardinal's mitre. Colonel Papa
le Bon was leaning on a pope's staff, a staff with a crucifix at the
top. Colonel Papa le Bon was carrying a bible in his left hand. To
top it all off, Colonel Papa le Bon was wearing an AK-47 slung
over his shoulder. The AK-47 and Papa le Bon were inseparable,
he carried it round with him night and day. That was on account
of the tribal wars. (Kourouma 52)

The constant repetition of "Papa le Bon," together with the details about his clothes, creates a picture of an almost impossibly
contradictory character, part priest, part butcher. With a leader
like this, the narrative suggests, there is no possibility of certitude.
In another scene, the narrator describes Papa le Bon's effective
moneymaking schemes. Le Bon's recruits hold up cars, kill their
occupants, steal their possessions, and hand them over to him.
Le Bon organizes activities like these, the narrator states, because
"That's the way it's supposed to happen. Because Colonel Papa le
Bon is the representative spokesman of the NPFL (the National
Patriotic Front of Liberia). The NPFL is the movement of the
warlord [Charles] Taylor, who wreaks havoc all over the region"
(47–48). The cynical tone here implies that being Taylor's sidekick
is all the reason le Bon needs for his murderous activities.

As often as the narrator speaks with the voice of a cynical
adult, he also articulates his childlike fears. Trauma specialist Boris
Cyrulnik has suggested that traumatized children often cope with
trauma by creating a strategy that uses "every resource to face the
danger" (26). Yet in Kourouma's narrative, Birahima uses every
resource he has to produce cynical asides and wry humor about the
war. In one scene, when a child soldier his age pushes a gun into
Birahima's bottom, the narrator reveals that he was "trembling,
trembling like the hindquarters of a nanny-goat waiting for a billy-
goat ('hindquarters' means 'arse, bum'). I felt like I needed to do

pee-pee, to do pooh, to do everything. Walahé!" (50–51). Later, when Birahima is forced to abandon two of his friends, Sarah and Kik, who have been injured by land mines and bullets, the narrator says: "We left Kik to the mercy of humans in the village the way we left Sarah to the mercy of the animals and the insects. Which of them was better off? Definitely not Kik. That's wars for you. Animals have more mercy for the wounded than humans" (89).

The narrator's voice is not just an unpredictable blend of adult cynicism and childlike fears. He repeatedly draws our attention to his obsession with dictionaries as a way of underscoring the futility of our own search for meaning within his narrative. The narrator tells us, early on, that Birahima always carries several dictionaries with him, including the *Larousse,* the *Petit Robert, The Glossary of French Lexical Peculiarities in Black Africa,* and the *Harrap's* (3). The narrator uses these resources to simultaneously explain and critique Côte d'Ivoire's cultural context for a Western reader. For example, when describing the magic charm that the healer who tried to cure Birahima's mother of her disability always carried with him, the narrator says: "(According to the *Glossary,* a 'grigri' is 'a protective amulet, often a piece of paper inscribed with magical incantation kept in a small leather purse which is tied above the elbow or around the neck')" (8). Here the narrator is satirizing Birahima's admiration for both traditional wisdom and the colonial educational system (Coundouriotis, "Arrested Historicization" 200).

In scenes like these, not only is the narrator's use of language highly artificial (201), but he constantly draws our attention to that fact. In doing so, he implies that child soldiers like himself, who end up writing novels, can only do so using "invented discourse(s)" (203). He writes: "Allah is not obliged to be fair about everything, about all his creations, about all his actions here on earth. The same goes for me. I don't have to talk, I'm not obliged to tell my dog's life-story, wading through dictionary after dictionary. I'm fed up talking" (Kourouma 91). Despite his desire to remain silent, the narrator suggests that writing about combat is actually a "brilliant idea" because it enables him to use "clever French words . . . big Black Nigger African Native words, and bastard nigger pidgin words. . . . The full, final and completely complete title of my bullshit story is: Allah is not obliged to be fair about all the things he does here on earth" (214–215). This ambiguous remark, with the narrative ending where it began (these are the exact words of the novel's opening paragraph), suggests that despite all its absurdities, Birahima's story will constantly reinvent itself.

Unlike *Allah Is Not Obliged, Johnny Mad Dog* is not a story that keeps reinventing itself. The narrative is based partly on Dongala's experiences of fleeing his home in Brazzaville during the civil war in the Republic of Congo (1997–2000) and hiding in the jungle. His house was fired on and actual child soldiers like Johnny, with machine guns, looted it and killed his friends and family. Unsurprisingly, therefore, *Johnny Mad Dog* is a remarkable depiction of the enduring effects of violence on children. In this, it straddles the African war novel and the African child soldier novel (Coundouriotis, *People's Right* 222). Unlike *Allah Is Not Obliged* and *Beasts of No Nation,* it has two sixteen-year-old narrators, Laokolé and Johnny, both of whom describe the effects of civil war on an unnamed country that resembles the Republic of Congo. Laokolé is a young Mayi-Dogo girl (the Mayi-Dogo being Dongala's fictional equivalent of Congolese loyalists, the group that, during the civil war, were loyal to President Lissouba). Johnny is a young Dogo-Mayi boy (the Dogo-Mayi being Dongala's fictional equivalent of Congolese rebels, the group that, during the civil war, were loyal to rebel leader Sassou-Nguesso). Laokolé makes constant references to her family, particularly her dead father, her handicapped mother, and her traumatized brother. Johnny describes, primarily, his militia unit and his gun. Although the two narrators alternate throughout the narrative, eventually, as Odile Cazenave suggests, Laokolé dominates. Even so, each narrator echoes the other, to the point where both "the oppressor and the victim live the same situation" (62–63).

On the surface, the two narrators present diametrically opposing viewpoints about war. Yet both narrators also constantly undermine their own positions. Johnny confesses, early on, that he was attracted to combat not because he liked violence but because was susceptible to the rhetoric of "intellectuals." Yet after he becomes a soldier, he learns how to enjoy killing and raping innocent civilians. By contrast, Laokolé, who is an intellectual in the making rather than a fake intellectual like Johnny (she was poised to study engineering before the war), is extremely protective of her mother and brother. Despite these differences, both narrators underscore the similarities in their backgrounds, indicating, for example, that both grew up in very poor households (Coundouriotis, *People's Right* 222).

Johnny describes his own aptitude for violence quite graphically, providing numerous examples of his killing and raping civilians just because he can. In one scene, Johnny describes his brutal rape of TT, a beautiful TV news anchor, thinking as he does so: "She was classy; I respected her. I'd never dreamed that someday I'd be doing this with her. I wished the TV cameras had been on" (Dongala 24–25). Throughout the narrative, Johnny presents himself not just as a bully, but as a confused and insecure one, such as when he measures his own incomplete education against the intellectuals he admires. He says, "I had great respect for them [intellectuals]. They had impressive diplomas and spoke flawless French; they were more intelligent than politicians. . . . Some of them had libraries where books were piled up to the ceiling" (87). In another scene, Johnny describes his excitement when he has a

wealthy couple, Mr. and Mrs. Ibara, in his power. Instead of killing them, however, Johnny feels the urge to prove his intellectual
prowess by asking them math questions (233). It is only when Mrs.
Ibara shows no fear that Johnny decides to rape her. He says, "For
the first time in my life, I was fucking an intellectual. I felt more
intelligent" (237). These constant shifts between descriptions of
gratuitous violence and his admiration for intellectuals underscore
his ruthlessness and immaturity as a soldier.

Early in his narrative, Johnny changes his name so that he can
measure up to the standards of ruthlessness he has set for himself.
Describing his new name, Johnny says that it is a "strong, powerful
name. A name that inspires the same gut-wrenching terror that a
condemned man feels before the firing squad, a name that makes
people tremble" (98). Yet soon after he acquires his new nom de
guerre, he becomes quite confused by the courage his potential
victims show. In one scene, when his unit tries to take over the UN
compound in the capital city, Johnny says, "To my great surprise
they [the UN staff] didn't run off, the way they had in Rwanda.
On the contrary, their Pakistani leader began to shout in English
. . . the guy . . . was mad as hell. I was caught up short. I didn't have
any backup plan" (130). In fact, he is even more surprised when
he realizes that other UN jeeps and soldiers have crept up behind
him, forcing him to beat a hasty retreat (132). In all these incidents
Johnny undercuts his presentation of his own ruthlessness with
images of his insecurities.

Toward the end of the narrative, Johnny describes a final showdown between himself and Laokolé. Despite Johnny's ruthlessness,
Laokolé incapacitates him by throwing a heavy Bible into his face.
Johnny describes his last thoughts as follows: "I fell over backward
from the blow. The nape of my neck smashed against the edge of
the table, and I landed on the floor, stunned, bleeding profusely .
. . a heavy object came smashing down on my fingers. And then a

fury began giving me relentless, repeated blows between my legs. The pain was unbearable" (317). The fact that Johnny narrates his dying thoughts makes the overtly religious overtones to this scene somewhat less significant. Moreover, like the narration of many other scenes in the novel, it also omits larger sociocultural issues and focuses completely on Johnny's final anguish (Coundouriotis, "Arrested Historicization" 200).

Just as Johnny undercuts descriptions of his own cruelty, Laokolé contrasts her compassion for others with her single-minded pursuit of her goals. Early scenes of the novel show Laokolé rescuing people adversely affected by the war, keeping them safe from harm. When her mother experiences a lot of pain, for example, Laokolé persuades a UN doctor to treat her (137). Later, however, when she sees the other refugees fighting for water from a tap in the UN compound, she becomes adept at street fighting: "I shoved, pulled, and stepped on people; I was shoved, pulled, and stepped on in turn. . . . A woman stuck out her foot and tripped me; I got up immediately and gave her a jab in the ribs . . . and thrust my jug under the spigot. I'd done it!" (139). Later in the narrative, when a stranger goes out of his way to help her, Laokolé thinks: "How was it possible that good could still exist in this world? I've often asked myself this question, and to this day it remains a puzzle to me" (244). Much later in the narrative, after being unable to prevent the deaths of her mother and friends, and having become a refugee herself, she finds a way out of this puzzle. Laokolé describes her attempts to entertain children in the refugee camp by teaching them to sing, and this action brings the refugees together in unexpected ways: "The kids had forgotten the dreary camp in which they were stagnating. They had become children once more . . . if I was happy, their parents were even happier" (298).

Laokolé provides many examples of her fierce loyalty to her family. In one scene, a departing foreign journalist offers Laokolé a chance to escape the carnage and move to Europe, but she refuses, saying: "No, I couldn't go. I couldn't leave Mama by herself, or Fofo either . . . I didn't want to leave the country if it meant leaving Mama and Fofo behind" (159–169). Yet several scenes later, Laokolé suggests that her commitment to her family has cut her off from the larger community that surrounds her. Describing her reactions as she watches Euronews' TV coverage of the carnage she has just witnessed, Laokolé says: "That young woman was me! That idiot, that blockhead who stood there so stupidly, like a cow watching a train go by—that was me, and I hadn't even recognized myself! It was the weirdest feeling" (211). By emphasizing her inability to recognize herself on TV, Laokolé suggests that she is troubled by the alienating representation of international news. Laokolé emphasizes her sense of dislocation for the remainder of the narrative, with detailed descriptions of her wanderings in the countryside in search of a sense of place. She spends a few days in a forest, befriends villagers, finds a refugee camp, and eventually kills Johnny. While the showdown between Laokolé and Johnny leaves us with the impression that Laokolé will be a ruggedly individual survivor, Laokolé suggests otherwise. Right after the showdown scene Laokolé hints that she will only survive if she can create a new family for herself, one that is also closely connected to the larger community. Laokolé goes on to adopt a war orphan and even has a naming ceremony for her. Laokolé says: "I sent my memory plunging into the rich heritage of my father's language, and I came up with the purest word of the tribe, the most beautiful word, a perfect reflection of the moment: Kiessé! Joy! My child, I name you Kiessé!" (320–321). This description suggests that Laokolé's ability to look both inward (toward her old family) and outward (toward the larger community) will help her survive both inside and outside a postwar community.

Somewhat less structured and layered than *Johnny Mad Dog,*

Beasts of No Nation was inspired by Iweala's readings about African child soldiers.[3] It was his first novel and he was only twenty-two when he wrote it. He was also inspired to write it after he met China Keitetsi. In an interview, Iweala claims that it was very hard for him to write the novel: "It was not a fun subject to deal with. Primarily because you're reading about tons and tons of atrocities committed, and the people who are doing them are younger than you. To spend so much time with violence in general—I was not very happy for the majority of time I was trying to write this" (Sachs). Iweala's protagonist, Agu, narrates the story using an involved first-person style, and his story unfolds in an unnamed nation that resembles Nigeria in the 1960s during its civil war.

Agu's first-person narration, like Mene's in *Sozaboy,* uses an invented language that is neither Nigerian pidgin nor Standard English. Comprising primarily interior monologues, this invented language has several peculiarities including the overuse of the present continuous tense, the omission of articles, and the incorrect pluralization of nouns (Kearney 80). Several interior monologues take us back to the past, before the war began. The narrator writes: "If I am closing my eye, I am seeing the rainy season and how, in my village, they are saying it is always bringing change too fast. You can be starting in one place with one plan and then finding that the whole world is washing away beneath your feets" (Iweala 57). In another scene, the narrator describes the prewar adventures of a hungry cloth seller, saying: "Normal, this man is not really helping to anybody and just trying to help himself, but this time he is hungrying so much that he is listening well well" (97). Later, the narrator confesses that he really likes attending school and that he was doing well "until the war is coming and then they are stopping school because there is no more government" (Iweala 27–29). The present continuous tense ("you can be starting," "he is hungrying," "they are stopping"), coupled with the incorrect pluralization ("feets"), makes his descriptions quite vivid. They also suggest that Agu had close ties to his community before the war.

During the war, the narrator describes how rebels (Iweala's fictional equivalent of Biafran soldiers) attack ten-year-old Agu's village, separating him from his family and community and forcing him to become a soldier. This part of the narrative traces Agu's movement from innocence to bestiality, and this trajectory is also implied in the novel's title. Yet the narrator seems less interested in Agu's transition from civilian to soldier than he is with the nature of combat itself, which becomes, for Agu as for other West African children, "a total condition, a way of life, not a cause in the name of something" (Coundouriotis, "Arrested Historicization" 196). This totalizing vision of war is maintained via the narrator's sustained use of animal imagery. In one scene, when Agu's commandant for the first time forces him to kill a federal soldier, and the frightened man loses control of his bowel movements, the narrator compares him to a goat on the chopping block (Iweala 20). Soon after, the killing itself becomes not just the death of one civilian but an act that affects the whole community. The narrator says, "The world is moving so slowly and I am seeing each drop of blood and each drop of sweat flying here and there. I am hearing the bird flapping their wing as they are leaving all the tree. It is sounding like thunder" (21).

The narrator's emphasis on the totalizing impact of war is sustained throughout the narrative. In one scene, the narrator describes a young girl whose hand has just been severed, just like Kamara's hand was cut off in *The Bite of the Mango*. He writes: "She is not screaming or shouting or making any noise. She is just having no more hand. Commandant is saying that she is enemy, she is stealing our food, and killing my family because she is enemy. I am jumping on her chest" (51). In *The Bite of the Mango,* the narrator described the mutilation by comparing Kamara's hand to a fish being chopped up; here, the narrator focuses on the girl as an object, dehumanizing her so that he can block off his emotions. Later, the narrator applies this dehumanizing technique to himself, when his own commanding officer sexually abuses him. He says: "He was entering inside of me the way the man goat is sometimes mistaking other man goat for woman goat and going inside of them" (Iweala 85).

In later sections of the novel, the narrator describes combat as an animal that is out of control: "I am not seeing road or village or woman or children for too long. I am only seeing war, one evil spirit sitting in the bush just having too much happiness because all the time he is eating what he wants to eat—us" (118). Even after Agu escapes, the narrator uses animal imagery to describe his experiences; however, the imagery becomes more abstract. Agu's journey (to recovery and a new life) now takes on beastly manifestations. As he walks, Agu notices that the road is "rising up and down like one animal . . . it is moving with the land that it is sitting on . . . because we are not respecting road from going to toilet and spitting everywhere on it, I am fearing that it may be killing us soon" (129). The imagery suggests that the path to recovery may be tortuous and may never end, consuming soldier and civilian alike. As Iweala suggested in an interview, he left the novel open-ended in order to leave unanswered such important questions as "What needs to be done to heal this child? Who is really responsible for the violence he committed? Who can even hope to understand?" (Smith).

One of the few points in the narrative when animal imagery is not used is the scene of Strika's death. Strika, Agu's friend and fellow child soldier, copes with his trauma by remaining mute throughout the narrative, much like young My Luck does in *A Song for Night* and little Citizen does in *Moses, Citizen, and Me.* Yet despite his apparent inability to show his emotions, Strika proves his loyalty to Agu on many occasions. When Strika dies, therefore, the narrator describes his death using language that humanizes him and calls attention to his suffering: "All of his skin is just coming away, and his eye is rolling up into his head and showing yellow and red everywhere like going to toilet and blood. . . . Strika is my brother and my family and the only person I can be talking to even if he is never talking back. . . . He is not saying anything" (Iweala 131–132). Other than this scene, the narrator's use of imagery suggests the endless tedium of war that constantly surrounds children like Agu.

All three novels depict children's experiences of war as horrifying and brutalizing, and describe conflict as a condition that disconnects them from their communities. The narratives are characterized by opposing sets of images that undermine each other (good and evil, innocence and corruption, idealism and cynicism). These fictional contradictions mimic the realities of the lives of young people all across Africa from the mid-twentieth century onward, whose social and political activities in the public arena were, as Mamadou Diouf points out, marginalized and stifled ("Afterword" 229). In the revolutions and dictatorships that sprang up all over sub-Saharan Africa in the latter half of the twentieth century and beyond, young Africans were displaced from the central spaces that they occupied in their societies to the extent that they were eventually marginalized, "feared, calumniated and avoided" (230). Like their real-life counterparts, the fictional child soldiers experienced various forms of "quiet marginalization" (Bolten 506) as their life experiences quickly erased the spaces between adolescence and childhood (Diouf, "Engaging," 9). Both Kourouma and Iweala had read about child soldiers fighting in West Africa and used those insights to develop their characterizations of Birahima and Agu. Kourouma often includes topical references to contemporary warlords, therefore, in scenes of *Allah*

Is Not Obliged. Birahima mentions what it was like to meet Charles
Taylor and Samuel Doe. While Iweala was a creative writing student at Harvard, China Keitetsi came to speak on his campus, and
he went to listen to her. That moved him to start writing a story
about a child soldier like Agu, a project that he finished after he
won a fellowship to study in Nigeria. He supplemented that study-
abroad experience with readings from human rights organizations, also incorporating insights from his father's experiences as
a nineteen-year-old guerrilla in the Nigerian civil war during the
late 1960s (Smith 1–2). Despite these "real life" elements within
both narratives, Agu and Birahima have their most memorable and
intense ethical debates with themselves. Both narratives include
numerous interior monologues, including oft-repeated words and
phrases, and the narrative voices are ironic and cynical. Dongala,
a well-established chemistry professor in the Republic of Congo,
had to flee for his life during his country's civil war, and he saw his
friends and acquaintances shot by teenagers carrying guns. That
led him to ask himself, "Where do they [the child soldiers] come
from? I mean, have they no parents? What kind of society brings up
kids like that?" (Valdes 27). In 1999, he traveled on a Guggenheim
fellowship all over Africa to do the research needed for the novel
(Anyinefa 98), and *Johnny Mad Dog* was published in French three
years later. It received good reviews in Spain and France, but its
North American reviewers found Johnny's character somewhat
overdone (Valdes 27). Shot through with fictional contradictions
coupled with realistic, topical references, *Johnny Mad Dog, Allah Is
Not Obliged,* and *Beasts of No Nation,* mark themselves off as child
soldier novels, not war novels, which typically remained grounded
within their community.

CHAPTER 5

Fictional Dystopias
in Child Soldier Narratives

A great change for the worse came over Chaka, both in his appearance and in his inner nature, in his purposes and his acts. In
the first place, all signs of kindness still left in him disappeared in
the terrible blackness of his heart. He could no longer distinguish
between war and murder; he regarded both in the same light.
And secondly, his real self died completely, a spirit more animal
than human took full possession of him.

> —Thomas Mofolo, *Chaka the Zulu*

D escribing the difficulties of being an African writer living in
the West, Delia Jarrett-Macauley once said in an interview
with Ambrose Musiyiwa: "[When you] write from the
inside . . . there are bound to be new challenging elements, but it
is important to write nevertheless without footnoting, without
patronizing and without debasing oneself to the level of meaningless generalizations" (Musiyiwa). When writers who are trying to
write from the "inside" write about children and violence, they
must deal with issues of ethics and values, including economic ones
(Neale 432). In this chapter, I will analyze Sierra Leonean–British

Delia Jarrett-Macauley's *Moses, Citizen, and Me* (2005), Nigerian-American Chimamanda Ngozi Adichie's *Half of a Yellow Sun* (2006), and Nigerian-British Chris Abani's *Song for Night* (2007). Characterized by dystopian imagery and nightmarish settings, these three novels about child soldiers couldn't be more different from those described in my previous chapter, despite being published soon after them. In *Moses, Citizen, and Me,* protagonist Julia can only imagine the lives of Sierra Leonean child soldiers like Citizen by having them inhabit, literally, the inside of her head. In this imaginary world inside Julia's head, Citizen is cured of his trauma and learns how to speak again. Ugwu, the child protagonist of *Half of a Yellow Sun,* experiences combat only briefly, but that exposure is enough for him to suffer from nightmares about rape and mutilation. Articulate and intelligent, Ugwu attempts to write about his experiences, but his narrative remains incomplete at the end. My Luck, the teenaged protagonist and narrator of *Song for Night,* speaks to us from the land of the dead. Using a voice we cannot hear, inside a body that feels pain and hunger, he inhabits a liminal space. These three novels use circular narratives, dystopic imagery, and affective registers to represent the ethics and values of war trauma.

According to critic Ananya Kabir, an effective way to represent traumatic wartime experiences is to connect them to dance and music (71).[1] Writing about the *kuduro,* a vigorous Angolan street dance performed by young men, Kabir argues that it has a subversive connection to Angola's traumatized past. This is because the dancers, who are typically from underprivileged backgrounds, engage in "dexterous language play, outrageous style statements, and names that draw on the two sources of power in contemporary Angola—oil and political status" (70). Although the *kuduro* makes no obvious references to Angola's civil wars of the 1980s and 1990s, it nevertheless reflects, according to Kabir, the successes and failures, optimism and despair of postwar Angola (70). Therefore, in order to understand the trauma of Angola's war years, one must also come to terms with the *kuduro.*

Other critics have analyzed representations of war by linking it to affect, to the body, and to place. As Judith Butler suggests, "What we feel is in part conditioned by how we interpret the world around us; and how we interpret what we feel actually can and does alter the feeling itself" (41). By this she means that our affective reactions to moments of horror are often "framed" by "interpretive schemes" we don't always understand. Therefore, we may experience horror during one moment of violence and may be indifferent during another (41). Butler argues that this difference in affective responses to violence (displayed most obviously in the United States during the post-9/11 era) is due to our tendency to divide human lives into those that are "worth defending, valuing, and grieving when they are lost" and those that are "not quite lives, not quite valuable, recognizable, or, indeed, mournable" (42–43). Therefore, how we choose to make those divisions will also condition our affective responses to trauma.

All three of the novels examined in this chapter present the lives of young African children as "mournable." Sierra Leonean expatriate Julia, the narrator of *Moses, Citizen, and Me,* leaves her home in England to help her extended family. In Freetown, she learns that eight-year-old Citizen, who was recruited by the RUF, brutally murdered Adele, his loving grandmother, and then became a street kid. Citizen appears, to her Anglicized eyes, physically and emotionally ill. When she meets others like him in a camp for former child soldiers in Freetown, she realizes that the war has warped their bodies, too. One camp inhabitant's face, she writes, was "missing; his nose slanted to one side and his teeth chattered by themselves"; while another boy's back from "neck to waistline" has "a bluish-purple gash [that] festered in the heat"

(Jarrett-Macauley 32). Although Citizen does not live in that camp, his disabilities are noticeable. Julia realizes, with a shock, that he cannot speak, producing instead sounds that are "nothing we could make sense of, no actual words—just noises and grunts [and] . . . a guff, guff noise, the sounds of a voiceless or wild creature" (42). In another scene, she finds out that after he had killed his grandmother, his hands shrank till they became "so small" that he "could never pull a trigger again" and all weapons "fell from [his] . . . hands" (220). Concerned about Citizen's traumatized state, Julia spends most of the narrative describing her attempts to form what Anne Whitehead has called an "adoptive maternal bond" with him (242). When these attempts fail, she creates a space inside her head where Citizen can express himself via performance and can bond with his peers. As my subsequent paragraphs will show, Julia links Citizen's trauma not just to his body but also to performance, thereby making his tragedy eminently "mournable."

Much of Julia's narration involves dream visions that take place inside her head, during which she travels to the rain forests of Sierra Leone, near the Liberian border, where many units of the RUF had once operated (Whitehead 252). As Whitehead suggests (253), it is Anita, a neighbor, who first "transports" Julia to this forested borderland via her act of braiding Julia's hair the Sierra Leonean way. Soon after the braiding begins, Julia realizes that her head has become "a map of Sierra Leone, its farmland, diamond mines, mountains, ridges, people, soldiers, fighters, leaders. Up the smooth dark skin of my neck marched a band of boy and girl soldiers" (Jarrett-Macauley 51). One of these marching soldiers is Citizen, attached to Lieutenant Ibrahim's "number-one-burn-house unit" in Julia's head, performing an endless routine of looting, killing, and raping: "After hunger, no proper food. After fighting, no rest" (58). As Julia watches, horrified, they attack villages, kill the innocent and disabled, and shoot drugs into their bodies.

Some of Julia's dream visions include encounters with the shaman-like Bemba G in Gola Forest, located deep within Sierra Leone's northern rain forest. As Julia watches, Bemba G turns his forest compound into a rehabilitation camp and welcomes former child soldiers of all shapes and sizes. Completely unfazed by their weapons and aggressive behavior, he devises daily activities involving mathematical games, storytelling, and dramatic performances, all of which slowly "transform" the children into a "cohesive group" that is "finally ready to move . . . back into the wider community" (Whitehead 253). One aspect of the children's transformation that Julia learns to appreciate is Bemba G's "reclaiming" of Sierra Leonean cultural practices that the war had destroyed. In particular, Bemba G takes over former RUF military camps and fills them with songs, dances, and stories. While there, he provides the children with feasts of traditional Sierra Leonean food that he has cooked from ingredients he has grown himself, such as cassava and black-eyed beans (Jarrett-Macauley 128–129). While the children relish the food, he tells them folk stories about talking trees and spider-like men (134) and organizes activities involving numbers and symbols that enhance the children's mathematical and social skills (91–92). Julia points out that often Bemba G follows a lesson on trigonometry with a dance session, underscoring the importance of community and the links between trauma and performance.

Performance is, in fact, one of Bemba G's most effective transformative tools. As Julia indicates, he encourages the children to perform Sierra Leonean playwright Thomas Decker's 1964 play *Juliohs Siza*. A translation of Shakespeare's *Julius Caesar* into Krio,[2] this play focuses on the problems that can occur when newly democratic African countries fail to prevent one-party dictatorships from emerging (255). Encouraging the children to perform in a medium that is grounded in their own political realities, Julia learns, helps them take pride in "the value of Sierra-Leonean culture and resources" (Whitehead 255). As she watches the children become familiar with the play, Julia notices that Bemba G allows rehearsals to stop whenever they want to talk about their experiences in combat (152–153). Despite all their stops and starts, including an intervention to prevent the older boys from making the fight sequences too realistic, the children perform the play successfully, in front of an audience, right in the forest. During the performance, Julia observes Citizen getting very nervous. Although Citizen is playing Brutus's servant and has specific lines to speak, Bemba G allows him to replace his lines with a Malian love song (181). When it's his turn to perform, Citizen sings that love song beautifully, falls asleep, dreams of a loving ghost with "naked brown arms" and a "back torn with wounds from a cruel death" (208), and wakes up shouting "Grandma!" (212). While Citizen and the other young children realize that, as they perform, "something else" is being transmitted to them (159), the older children understand, instinctively, that they are "meeting themselves in the play" (159).

At the end of Julia's narrative, Citizen is partially reintegrated with his family, and Julia herself is poised to leave for home. Bemba G's other children also find real communities they can return to. As for the other children in narrative, including some that remain in the camps for war orphans, mentioned earlier in this chapter, they remain largely excluded from the larger Freetown community. However, their narratives remain "mournable" both inside and outside of Julia's head, and their stories are not forgotten. In this way, Julia's narrative within *Moses, Citizen, and Me* represents the affective registers of trauma and enables traumatized children like Citizen to express themselves in performance.

Like Citizen, thirteen-year-old Uwgu in Adichie's *Half of a Yellow Sun* is forced to become a soldier during Nigeria's civil war. Because she had no direct contact with that war (Anyokwu

179), Adichie read thirty-one books written by Nigerians who had experienced the war and interviewed many of her family members. Set in southeastern Nigeria during the early and late 1960s, *Half of a Yellow Sun* uses an omniscient narrative style. According to Eleni Coundouriotis, it is partly a child soldier novel and partly a "feminized war novel" with a focus on the history of the ordinary people (*People's Right* 225). This is because the omniscient narrator focuses on two protagonists, Ugwu and Olanna. Ugwu, who grew up in rural poverty and goes to work in cities like Nsukka and Enugu, eventually becomes Odenigbo's trusted servant. Olanna, whose parents are extremely wealthy, lives and works in Nsukka, Port Harcourt, and other cities, with her lover Odenigbo, her twin Kainene, Kainene's lover Richard, and a wide circle of friends. Although the narrator contrasts Ugwu's perspective as a barely literate boy from the village with that of his well-educated employers, the focus is on Ugwu's insights before and during the civil war.

In the early part of the narrative, the narrator describes Ugwu's work ethic and his academic aptitude. Once Odenigbo starts paying his school fees, he does very well at studies. Around the middle of the narrative, the civil war breaks out, and the narrator describes how Ugwu, along with Olanna and Odenigbo, moves from town to town to avoid bombardment by the federal army. It is not until three-quarters of the narrative is over, in chapter 29, that Ugwu is forcibly conscripted into the Biafran army. Unlike Citizen, however, Ugwu is more aware of what he is going through. In successive scenes, the narrator uses different affective registers to record Ugwu's reaction to war. In one scene, he detonates a land mine and is elated when it kills several Nigerian soldiers at once (371). In another scene, he is horrified to find out that his buddies are gang-raping a bar girl. When they notice him backing away, they challenge him to "prove his manhood." He ends up betraying "his own values" (Strehle 6678) by caving in to peer pressure and raping the bar girl brutally. As the rest of the narrative reveals, this violent episode haunts him for the rest of his life.

In other scenes, the omniscient narrator contrasts Ugwu's street smarts (such as his ability to recognize political propaganda) with his naivete (about issues like sexual violence and rape as a weapon of war). Before he is recruited, he only partly understands when his love interest, Eberechi, tells him how her parents had offered her up to an army colonel in exchange for a job for her brother. Yet her words also cause him anger and shame: "He felt angry that she had gone through what she had. . . . He thought, in the following days, about him and Eberechi in bed, how different it would be from her experience with the colonel. He would treat her with the respect she deserved" (300). After he is recruited, the shame and anger Eberechi's words had caused him merge with his memories of the rape of the bar girl, and he experiences guilt and remorse. The same mixture of emotions characterizes his realization that during the war, Anulika, his sister, and Nnesinachi, his teenage sweetheart, were both raped, often repeatedly, resulting in physical and psychological deformities. Describing Anulika's appearance several years after the gang rape, the narrator writes: "Her face was covered in blackheads and pimples and she . . . [was] not at all [beautiful]. She was an ugly stranger who squinted with one eye" (Adichie, *Half* 433). Later, Nnesinachi describes to Ugwu how she gave herself to a young Hausa soldier who was relatively kind to her, but who abandoned her after she became pregnant with his child (434). When Ugwu fully understands what both women have endured, all he can do is weep (434).

Toward the end of the narrative, the omniscient narrator describes Ugwu's emotions as he deals with the war's aftermath. In one scene, he listens, engrossed, as Richard (Kainene's British lover) describes a book he is writing about the war. He is haunted

by the book's title, *The World Was Silent When We Died,* because it
"filled him with shame. It made him think about that girl in the bar;
her pinched face and the hate in her eyes as she lay on her back on
the dirty floor" (406). During delirious spells as he recovers from
his injuries, he sees the bar and the girl on the floor again and again,
and the girl metamorphoses into Eberechi (407). The guilt he feels
propels him, as the narrator shows, to write about the human suffering the war has caused. At first a series of disconnected episodes
about the war, his chronicle later becomes a series of anecdotes
about the suffering of ordinary people. As Ugwu writes, however,
the narrator focuses more on his emotions than on the book's content. In one scene, Ugwu sits under a tree, writing, while children
play nearby. Ugwu notices that a child whose stomach had recently
become distended and whose skin had become discolored is no
longer with them. He feels the urge to explain to the remaining
children "what kwashiorkor was" (410) but decides against it. Instead, he recalls a time, earlier in the narrative, when he had saved
that child's life during a bomb assault. As that memory flits into his
head, he hears the child's mother wailing, presumably because the
child has just died of kwashiorkor. The episode ends with Ugwu's
reflections about the mother's emotions as she grieves her child's
death and provides few insights about what Ugwu will write about.
All we can surmise is that his chronicle will, as Pauline Uwakweh
argues, link to "other global voices on the atrocities of war, human
suffering, and resilience" (101).

   As the war peters out and Kainene disappears (she never
comes back from a trading mission), Richard declares that "the
war isn't my story to tell, really" (Adichie 438), and encourages
Ugwu to continue writing. Ugwu thereupon writes his narrative,
The World Was Silent When We Died, after which both the omniscient narrator and Ugwu end their narratives simultaneously. By
ending the narrative with a description of Ugwu's newly written

narrative, Adichie projects, in Coundouriotis' words, "the people's history beyond the end of the novel, when Ugwu will complete his book" (*People's Right* 227). More importantly, by linking writing and trauma in unique ways, the novel foregrounds the affective registers of Ugwu's war trauma.

Like *Half of a Yellow Sun, Song for Night* is also about the Nigerian civil war. The country itself is never named but seems to resemble Nigeria during the civil war, with Igbo-speaking rebels like protagonist My Luck fighting federal troops for control of the country. The narrator of this lyrical, stream-of-consciousness-style text is a dead child soldier who cannot speak. "What you hear is not my voice" (Abani 19), he says, after he is blown apart in a mine explosion. Unlike Citizen in *Moses, Citizen, and Me,* My Luck's muteness isn't a result of war trauma. He cannot speak because his vocal cords were cut in two when he was twelve. At that time, he was a mine scout and all mine scouts had their vocal cords severed so that they couldn't scream when they were blown to bits by land mines. My Luck communicates via interior monologues, which he sustains till the end of the narrative. At the end, when he reaches what appears to be his childhood home, he shouts out "Mother!" (167).

My Luck's interior narratives are not in English. As he claims near the outset, "My inner-speech is not in English . . . you are in fact hearing my thoughts in Igbo" (Abani 21). This thought-speech has taught him, he claims, alternative methods of communication. He says, "We [silenced mine scouts] have developed a crude way of talking, a sort of sign language that we have become fluent in. For instance, silence is a steady hand, palm flat, facing down" (19). Using his body as a narrative, he marks each comrade's death with incision into his arms, claiming, as he does so, that his arms are his "personal cemetery. I touch each cross, one for every loved one lost" (38).

My Luck's narrative is written partly on his body and partly by using distinctive imagery (Kearney 80). While some critics have read My Luck as "morally tormented" (85), others, like Kenneth Harrow, have suggested that his narrative is a return to the repressed memory of the traumatic rape and death of his mother. That traumatic episode, which he was forced to witness (Abani 3), becomes a point of deep silence within his interior monologues. He says: "I cannot name it, those things that happened while I watched, and I cannot speak something that was never in words, speak of things I cannot imagine, could never have seen even as I saw it" (43). This trauma, repressed in his memory, surfaces in his repeated references to death. In one of his asides he compares death to a river, reflecting, "I have cheated death's course many times and I am still here, like an undercurrent, full of a hate dark as any undertow" (46). In another scene, he comes across a group of old women in a village that has been devastated and abandoned. Although they have no food, they are cooking something in a large cauldron. As he approaches, he notices that the cauldron contains a "small arm ending in a tiny hand, and the tiny head still wearing its first down" (28). Despite being dead himself, he remains haunted, for the rest of the narrative, by the vision of the dead child's head, bobbing up and down in the cooking pot.

My Luck's narrative links war trauma to the body in ways that are less macabre, too. He describes an encounter with a group of severely injured villagers including "children without arms or legs or both, men with only half a face, women with shrapnel-chewed scars for breasts" (50). To his surprise, even the most disabled among them appear to be "holding onto life and hope with a fire that burned feverishly in their eyes" (50). Watching them he concludes that "if any light comes from this war, it will come from eyes such as those" (50). Unable to share their stubborn ability to hold onto hope, he fails to create a sense of community and continues with his wanderings.

My Luck's monologues link events in the present to memories from his past. In one scene, he remembers how he accidentally killed a child. When his platoon commander, John Wayne, boasts that he will rape a seven-year-old girl, My Look shoots him and kills the child too: "He [John Wayne] moved, instinctively I think, the way an animal will, to escape the shot, and the bullet went through the seven-year-old and found John Wayne's heart. They both looked at me, faces wide with shock" (41). Like the image of the child's head floating in the soup, this child's face haunts him and keeps surfacing in his memory.

In another scene, he finds an abandoned, run-down ambulance and suddenly remembers how his love interest, Ijeoma, died. Because she had stepped on a land mine, she "no longer had any arms or legs and wasn't much more than a bloody torso, lacerated by shrapnel, body parts scattered in a way that cannot be explained or described" (54). The ambulance triggers this memory because earlier in the war he and Ijeoma had run away together and had secretly lived inside that same ambulance for several months, eating whatever the forest provided and "making love with desperation tinged with the foreknowledge of loss" (58). As he realizes later, the only way he can deal with memories like these is by releasing them (104).

My Luck's contradictory, self-reflexive narrative style is quite unlike that of any of the other fictional child narrators. In one scene, he remembers an episode from his childhood when his grandfather tells him the creation story of his people, the Igbo. My Luck's grandfather describes how God created a female deity, Idemilli, to control man's excesses. Idemilli, his grandfather tells him, is a fiery being that contains the souls of the dead and that lives in a mysterious lake at the center of the universe. Kenneth

Harrow argues that Idemilli is Mami Wata, an unrepresentable being who causes death (14). When My Luck gets confused and complains he can't understand, his grandfather tells him: "Nobody does [understand]. Everybody does. It [the creation story] is real because it is a tall tale. This lake is the heart of our people. This lake is love. If you find it . . . you can climb it into the very heart of God. . . . It is at the center of you, because you are the world" (Abani 73). Later in the narrative, My Luck creates his own version of this creation story when he has a strange dream. In the dream, the hatred that he feels in his heart takes the form of a woman like Idemilli, filled with fire and ice, whose laughter is a literal vise around his heart, choking him to death. As he chokes he looks up at the sky and sees Ijeoma transformed into a star. However, her stellar beauty is quickly extinguished by the fiery woman of hatred, and she falls from the sky. As she falls, the vise around his heart is loosened and he can breathe again (Abani 87). The imagery of the dream suggests the power of love that he had noticed in the scene with the injured villagers with hopeful eyes is the only force in the world that will endure.

The hopefulness of My Luck's dream looks forward to the mysterious ending of the narrative, mentioned earlier, when My Luck finds his voice. After a perilous river crossing he encounters a woman who is a younger, happier version of his mother. "You are home" (167), she exclaims just as he realizes his voice has come back. While the water he crosses to get to his mother may not be mysterious as Idemilli's lake, nevertheless, its symbolism as a literal "river of death" (164) is obvious. Despite already being dead, My Luck must overcome his fear of death, understand the power of love, and reject hatred in order to find his mother.

Song for Night, like *Moses, Citizen, and Me,* and *Half of a Yellow Sun,* presents horrifying, dystopic landscapes of war, in which unspeakable traumas manifest themselves in the child soldier's

body and through his performance. While Citizen connects to a
new community through performance, Ugwu uses a newly written chronicle of war as a vehicle for his personal redemption. My
Luck, by contrast, never really finds a release from his pain, but
his silent, unspoken narrative acts as a form of redemption. Both
Julia and My Luck have visions and dreams that are nightmarish
and unreal. Julia cannot even empathize with child soldiers like
Citizen until she creates a space for them inside her head, while
My Luck starts his narrative with a description of his own death
and ends it with a rebirth of sorts. Ugwu never fully comprehends
the extent of the violence surrounding him. He dimly realizes that
his employer, Olanna, had escaped some of the early violence by
riding in a crowded train car next to a mother who is holding her
child's severed head in a calabash. However, the significance of that
memory is not clarified in the narrative until much later. As readers, our affective responses to these war narratives is determined
by what Butler calls a "tacit realization that there is a worthy life
that has been injured or lost in the context of war, and no utilitarian
calculus can supply the measure by which to gauge the destination
and loss of such lives" (54). Given that missing calculus to gauge
the losses of war, the texts themselves remain as proof of "stubborn life, vulnerable, overwhelmed . . . dispossessed" (62). Child
soldier narratives like these highlight the dystopic, nightmarish
scenarios that result when children become bloodthirsty soldiers.
The contradictory images, narrative gaps, and affective registers
within these narratives underscore the numerous ways in which
wars alienate and isolate African children, and prevent their voices
from being heard.

Notes

Chapter 1. War Narratives and African Children

1. Examples include Ngugi wa Thiong'o's *A Grain of Wheat* (1967), Chinua Achebe's *Girls at War* (1972), Flora Nwapa's *Never Again* (1975), Buchi Emecheta's *Destination Biafra* (1982), Chenjerai Hove's *Bones* (1988), Boubakar Boris Diop's *Murambi: The Book of Bones* (2000, 2006), Nuruddin Farah's *Links* (2004), and Maaza Mengiste's *Beneath the Lion's Gaze* (2010), to name just a few.

2. Although Myanmar/Burma has one of the highest rates of child soldier recruitment and there are child soldiers on every continent, the problem is acute in Africa (Gettleman 7). Between 2004 and 2007, the following African governments actively used child soldiers in armed conflict (as soldiers or as human shields): Chad, Democratic Republic of the Congo, Somalia, Sudan and Southern Sudan, the Central African Republic, and Uganda ("Child Soldiers" 16). And in the following African countries, children were used by paramilitaries or militias supported by governments: Chad, Côte d'Ivoire, Liberia, Sierra Leone, and Uganda (Gettleman 7). Between 2004 and 2005, the UN Security Council adopted two important resolutions, numbers 1539 and 1612, both of which called for the establishment of a

monitoring and reporting mechanism on children and armed conflict.
Now set up in around a dozen countries, the mechanism is tasked with
documenting six categories of grave abuse against children, including
recruitment and use of children in situations of armed conflict
("Child Soldiers" 14). Also, in 2008, the Optional Protocol to the
Convention on the Rights of the Child on the involvement of children
in armed conflict, the most specific prohibition of child soldiers under
international law, was ratified by 120 states (13).

3. As Honwana indicates, new child soldier recruits in southern and
Central Africa were often forced into continuous physical drills till
they reached physical exhaustion. They were also coerced into using
drugs like marijuana frequently, followed by severe beatings for minor
infractions. They were brutalized into committing horrific acts of
violence during their military training to make sure that they were
completely dehumanized. In most cases, attempts to escape were met
with death, so the new recruits lived in a constant state of terror (59).

4. As Slaughter puts it, "The Bildungsroman, the public sphere and the
democratic state are interdependent elements in the human rights
package" (149). Besides Slaughter and his work on the bildungsroman,
James Dawes has identified a subgenre of American literature that he
calls the "novel of human rights," which is both "inward and outward
looking" and which "imports" the "terms and methods of universal
human rights both to ethnic American literary studies and to the
specific historical and contemporary justice movements" ("Novel of
Human Rights" 134). Just as fictional narratives about human rights are
now considered to be a part of American literature, I would argue that
the African child soldier novel and the African child soldier memoir,
based as they are within the African war novel genre, are very much a
part of this global discourse on human rights.

5. Not all collaborative child soldier memoirs have been scrutinized
for veracity. For example, *They Poured Fire on Us from the Sky* was
written by three Sudanese Lost Boys: Benson Deng, Alephonsion

Deng, and Benjamin Ajak, together with American volunteer Judy A. Bernstein. It was widely praised for its sincerity and simplicity. Bernstein, who is the founder of the International Rescue Committee's Lost Boys Education Fund, met the three boys in 2001 and helped them write their memoir. The writing process took about four years ("Judy A. Bernstein"). The boys now regularly give speaking tours all over the United States, and their memoir has its own website: www. theypouredfire.com.

6. The conflicts described in *I, Rigoberta Menchú* between the Quiché community and Guatemalan landowners were part of a larger struggle over land that begin in the sixteenth century when Spanish conquistadors took over Guatemala and killed almost all the Mayan elite. In the 1970s the Alliance for Progress Party began to organize the Quiché people politically, forming, in 1973, the Committee for Peasant Unity. The brutal way in which its activists were treated forced it underground, and it later merged with the Guerrilla Army of the Poor, or EGP. In the early 1980s the Guatemalan army attacked the EGP's safe houses in Guatemala City and destroyed Mayan villages (Arias 4). By 1983 the EGP was destroyed. In the process, according to various UN reports, more than 450 Maya villages were destroyed, more than one hundred thousand people were killed, and more than a million refugees were created. Menchú herself escaped only by fleeing to Mexico. In the mid-1980s she gained recognition as a spokesperson for her grassroots political movement and, in 1982, she agreed to tell her story to Burgos-Debray (Arias 4–5).

7. Many of these theorists argued that trauma survivors suffer from "dissociative amnesia" (Bremner 220) and cannot remember precise details about their traumatic experiences (Piers 58). Instead, they use "somatic sensations, behavioral reenactments, nightmares, and flashbacks" (van der Kok and van der Hart 172). This focus on the ways that trauma survivors construct or fail to construct linear narratives is partly a result of the huge outpouring of narratives about the Jewish

Holocaust during World War II. So much attention was eventually placed on Holocaust stories that these became the "template for all forms of traumatic telling, response, and responsibility within the contemporary field of human rights" (Schaffer and Smith 20). Both factual accounts of the Holocaust, as well as fragmented and disjoined ones, were analyzed and circulated around the world. Schaffer and Smith offered many examples of such Holocaust memoirs, including those written by Elie Wiesel and Primo Levi, as well as movies like Claude Lanzmann's Shoah and Steven Spielberg's *Schindler's List* (236).

8. Lynn Walford, in her article "The Debate over Testimonial Writing," makes an extended comparison between *Fragments* and *I, Rigoberta Menchú*. She suggests that the biggest difference between the two memoirs is that the former is a "complete fabrication," while the latter is an embellishment or exaggerated version of events that did take place (119). This distinction, between fabrication (a narrative that is invented) and embellishment (a narrative that is invented but accompanies a narrative that is factually accurate) is an important one for my project.

Chapter 2. False Combat and Adolescent Life Writing

1. According to his own website, in 2007, Beah was appointed UNICEF's first Advocate for Children Affected by War; he later became a member of the Human Rights Watch Children's Rights Division Advisory Committee, and testified before the US Congress. Also in 2007, he founded the Ishmael Beah Foundation to help children affected by war, and in 2008 he cofounded the Network of Young People Affected by War. He has been interviewed by numerous news organizations and celebrities, including Voice of America and CNN (in 2012), Oprah Winfrey and Publisher's Weekly (in 2013), and USA

Today (in 2014). Both *A Long Way Gone* and his novel *Radiance of Tomorrow* (2014) were reviewed by major journals and newspapers, including the *New York Times* and *The Guardian* ("Ishmael Beah").

2. Sawaneh and Williams are fairly well known within humanitarian circles both in Sierra Leone and in the global public arena. Sawaneh became a child soldier at age ten when he was forced to fight with the Revolutionary United Front (RUF) in Sierra Leone. After two years, he was rescued in 2000, and in 2001, he became the first child to address the United Nations Security Council ("Alhaji"). Williams became a child soldier at age seven when he was also forced to fight for the RUF. He ended up fighting for six months with the RUF and for three years with the Sierra Leone army. In 1994, he was rescued by UNICEF and went on to finish college (McGregor). Both young men now give talks about their experiences all over the world.

Chapter 3. Combat as Backdrop in Young Adult Life Writing

1. In 1987, the civil war in Sudan caused about twenty thousand young boys (most of them aged six or seven) to flee from their families in southern Sudan. They walked to Ethiopia and then on to Kenya, a distance of more than one thousand miles, and half of them died on the way. The survivors became known as the Lost Boys of Sudan. In 2001, about four thousand Lost Boys were resettled in the United States ("The Lost Boys").

2. Grace Akallo was not the only girl who was kidnapped from St. Mary's College, Aboké. In fact, 138 other girls were kidnapped along with her, aged between twelve and fifteen. A Belgian journalist, Els de Temmerman, wrote a narrative about that mass kidnapping, *The Aboké Girls* (2000). In that narrative, Temmerman presents four points of view about the kidnapping: Sister Rachele's, the school's deputy headmistress, who followed the LRA rebels and negotiated

with them to get 109 of the 139 girls released; Ellen's and Sarah's, two of the kidnapped girls, who had to find their own way to freedom; and Norman's, a young LRA fighter, who kidnapped the girls. Ellen, Sarah, and Norman all eventually escaped.

3. As Joy Okech has shown, the sexual exploitation of girls and women by the LRA was widespread; moreover, according to Jennifer Moore, many such girls were ostracized upon their return to civilian society, not just because they were perceived as "impure," but also because their sexual enslavement was regarded, by civilians, as a form of "privilege" that prevented their deaths in captivity (219).

4. The movie's depiction of Auma's and Lanyero's postescape limited employment opportunities echoes the findings of several social scientists who interviewed women who had escaped sexual slavery by LRA commanders. Hovil and Lomo found that most of the women who had returned to their former communities were living in terrible conditions (17), while Patricia Atim reported that women who had returned to IDP camps were being subjected to violence and rape (193).

Chapter 4. Narrative Uncertainty in Child Soldier Fiction

1. In reality, child soldiers undergoing rehabilitation were often resistant to the idea that they were really innocent and frequently attacked caregivers who suggested as much (Coundouriotis, "Arrested Historicization" 192). The communities that real-life child soldiers came from often regarded them solely as perpetrators, and returning child soldiers were therefore often obsessed with "rituals of purification" (193), many of which did not include narrating or verbalizing their violent experiences (193).

2. Other novelists writing in French that have used child protagonists or voices are Gaston-Paul Effa, Boubacar Boris Diop, and Tierno

Monénembo, but their narratives offer some hope for the children at the end (Cazenave 62).

3. Ten years after *Beasts of No Nation* was published, a movie version of the story was produced, which became the first feature film to be distributed by Netflix simultaneously via its streaming service and in theaters (Bitel 59).

Chapter 5. Fictional Dystopias in Child Soldier Narratives

1. Dance and music emanating from trauma also characterize the output of Sierra Leone's Refugee All Stars, a musical group that works with the Red Cross and major music producers to recount "the struggles faced by refugees from around the world." Among other things, this group started a media production team named "We Own TV" that made public health-related announcements during the recent Ebola outbreak in Sierra Leone ("Sierra Leone's Refugee"). Also see Fine and Nix's film *War Dance* (2007).

2. Krio is a hybrid language spoken in Sierra Leone, created by freed American slaves, combining elements of English with West African languages. In the novel, the child soldiers themselves speak many languages besides English and Krio, such as Mende and Temne (Whitehead 256).

Bibliography

Abani, Chris. *Song for Night.* Brooklyn: Akashic Books, 2007.

"About Chosen Books." chosenbooks.com.

"About Ekstra Bladet Publishers." Ekstra Bladet Publishers. www. ekstrabladetsforlag.dk.

"About Groundviews." www.groundviews.org/about/.

"About" [Holtzbrinck Publishing Group]. www.holtzbrinck.com.

Achebe, Chinua. *Girls at War and Other Stories.* London: Heinemann, 1972.

Adichie, Chimamanda Ngozi. "A Brief Conversation with Chimamanda Ngozi Adichie." *World Literature Today* 80.2 (March-April 2006): 5–6.

———. *Half of a Yellow Sun.* Lagos: Farafina, 2006.

Akallo, Grace. "An African Tale, Continued: First Hell, Then College, Now a Journey to America." *Chronicle of Higher Education* 51.8 (October 15, 2004).

Akhtar, Salman, and Glenda Wrenn. "The Biopsychosocial Miracle of Human Resilience: An Overview." In *The Unbroken Soul: Tragedy, Trauma, and Human Resilience,* ed. Henri Parens, Harold P. Blum, and Salman Akhtar. Lanham, MD: Jason Aronson, 2008: pages 1–20.

"Alhaji Babah Sawaneh: Former Child Soldier at the Security Council." Office of the Special Representative of the Secretary

General for Children and Armed Conflict. March 13, 2014. childrenandarmedconflict.un.org.

Allen, Tim. *Trial Justice: The International Criminal Court and the Lord's Resistance Army.* London: Zed Books, 2006.

Andrews, William L. *To Tell a Free Story: The First Generation of Afro-American Autobiography, 1760–1865.* Urbana: University of Illinois Press, 1986.

Anyinefa, Koffi. "Emmanuel Dongala." *Dictionary of Literary Biography* 360. *Contemporary African Writers.* Ed. Tanure Ojaide. Detroit: Gale, 2011: pages 94–99.

Anyokwu, Christopher. "'May We Always Remember': Memory and Nationhood in Chimamanda Ngozi Adichie's *Half of a Yellow Sun.*" *NTU Studies in Language and Literature* 20 (December 2008): 179–196.

Appadurai, Arjun. *Modernity at Large: Cultural Dimensions of Globalization.* Minneapolis: University of Minnesota Press, 1996.

Arias, Arturo, ed. *The Rigoberta Menchú Controversy.* Minneapolis: University of Minnesota Press, 2001,

Atim, Patricia. "The Legal Regime Governing Sexual and Gender-Based Violence: A Case Study of Pajule Internally Displaced Peoples' Camp, Uganda." *East African Journal of Peace and Human Rights* 15.1 (January 2009): 186–217.

Atuhaire, Alex B. "China Keitetsi Tours Germany." *The Monitor* (Uganda) (February 8, 2003).

——. "Keitetsi to Release War Videos." *The Monitor* (Uganda) (May 20, 2003).

Auden, W. H. "Musée des Beaux Arts (1940)." *Poetry by Heart.* http://www.poetrybyheart.org.uk.

Batey, Angus. "'I Just Wanted to Kill': Emmanuel Jal Was a Child Soldier in Sudan. Now He's Using Rap to Preach against Gang Violence in Britain." *The Guardian* (April 8, 2008): 28.

Beah, Ishmael. *A Long Way Gone: Memoirs of a Boy Soldier.* New York:

Farrar, Straus & Giroux, 2007.

Berger, Roger A. "Decolonizing African Autobiography." *Research in African Literatures* 41.2 (Summer 2010): 32–54.

Beverley, John. "The Margin at the Center: on Testimonio (Testimonial Narrative)." In *The Real Thing: Testimonial Discourse and Latin America,* ed. Georg M. Gugelberger. Durham and London: Duke University Press, 1996: 23–41.

Bhabha, Homi K. "Making Difference: The Legacy of the Culture Wars." *Artforum International* (April 2003). www.artforum.com.

Bitel, Anton. "Beasts of No Nation." *Sight and Sound* (December 2015): 58–59.

Blunt, Sheryl Henderson. "The Devil's Yoke: A Young Woman Describes Her Former Life as a Slave of Rebel Soldiers." *Christianity Today* (March 2007): 39.

Bolten, Catherine. "'We Have Been Sensitized': Ex-Combatants, Marginalization, and Youth in Postwar Sierra Leone." *American Anthropologist* 114.3 (2012): 496–508.

Boulukos, George E. "Olaudah Equiano and the Eighteenth-Century Debate on Africa." *Eighteenth-Century Studies* 40.2 (Winter 2007): 241–255.

Boustany, Nora. "Emmanuel Jal: A Child of War, a Voice of Peace; a Sudanese 'Lost Boy' Hopes to Sing Away the Pain." *Washington Post* (January 6, 2008).

Boyd, Sarah. "Girl Soldier." *Dominion Post* (August 14, 2004).

Bremner, J. Douglas. "Traumatic Memories Lost and Found: Can Memories of Abuse Be Found in the Brain?" In *Trauma and Memory,* ed. Linda M. Williams and Victoria L. Banyard. Thousand Oaks, CA: Sage, 1999: pages 217–227.

Brown, DeNeen L. "A Child's Hell in the Lord's Resistance Army; Years after She Escaped Ugandan Rebels, Grace Akallo Fights to End a War." *Washington Post* (May 10, 2006).

Brown, Laura S. *Cultural Competence in Trauma Therapy: Beyond the*

Flashback. Washington, DC: American Psychological Association, 2008.

Butler, Judith. *Frames of War: When Is Life Grievable?* London: Verso, 2010.

Carroll, Steven. "Non-fiction" (review of Senait Mehari's *Heart of Fire*). *The Age* (Melbourne) (September 23, 2006).

Caruth, Cathy. *Unclaimed Experience: Trauma, Narrative, and History.* Baltimore: Johns Hopkins University Press, 1996.

Cazenave, Odile. "Writing the Child, Youth, and Violence into the Francophone Novel from Sub-Saharan Africa: The Impact of Age and Gender." *Research in African Literatures* 36.2 (Summer 2005): 59–71.

Caton, Hilary. "Mariatu Kamara Tells Burlington Crowd Heartfelt Story of Life in Sierra Leone." *Burlington Post* (March 11, 2014).

"Child Soldiers Global Report 2008." Coalition to Stop the Use of Child Soldiers, London, 2008.

Clarke, Cath. "The Guardian: First Sight Letekidan Micael." *The Guardian* (London) (August 21, 2009).

"Company History." Verlagscruppe Georg von Holtzbrinck GmbH. www.holtzbrinck.com. July 11, 2013.

"Controversial Child Soldier Film Shown at Berlin." Deutsche Press-Agentur (February 14, 2008).

Coundouriotis, Eleni. "The Child Soldier Narrative and the Problem of Arrested Historicization." *Journal of Human Rights* 9 (2010): 191–206.

——— . *The People's Right to the Novel: War Fiction in the Postcolony.* New York: Fordham University Press, 2014.

Craps, Stef. "Beyond Eurocentrism: Trauma Theory in the Global Age." In *The Future of Trauma Theory,* ed. Gert Buelens, Sam Durrant, and Robert Eaglestone. London: Routledge / Taylor & Francis, 2014: pages 45–61.

——— . "On Not Closing the Loop: Empathy, Ethics, and Transcultural Witnessing." In *The Postcolonial World,* ed. Jyotsna G. Singh and David D. Kim. London: Routledge / Taylor & Francis, 2017: pages 53–62.

Cyrulnik, Boris. "Children in War and Their Resiliences." In *The Unbroken Soul: Tragedy, Trauma, and Human Resilience,* ed. Henri Parens, Harold P. Blum, and Salman Akhtar. Lanham, MD: Jason Aronson / Rowman & Littlefield, 2008: pages 21–36.

Dallaire, Roméo, with Jessica Dee Humphreys. *They Fight Like Soldiers, They Die Like Children: The Global Quest to Eradicate the Use of Child Soldiers.* New York: Walker, 2010.

Dawes, James. "Human Rights in Literary Studies." *Human Rights Quarterly* 31.2 (May 2009): 394–409.

——. "The Novel of Human Rights." *American Literature* 88.1 (March 2016): 127–157.

De Boeck, Filip, and Alcinda Honwana. "Introduction: Children and Youth in Africa: Agency, Identity and Place." In *Makers and Breakers: Children and Youth in Postcolonial Africa,* ed. Alcinda Honwana and Filp de Boeck. Oxford: James Currey; Trenton, NJ: Africa World Press, 2005: pages 1–18.

Deng, Benson, Alephonsion Deng, and Benjamin Ajak. *They Poured Fire on Us from the Sky: The True Story of Three Lost Boys from Sudan.* New York: Public Affairs, 2005.

Denov, Myriam. *Child Soldiers: Sierra Leone's Revolutionary United Front.* Cambridge: Cambridge University Press, 2010.

Denselow, Robin. "Film and Music: Jazz, World, Folk, etc: Emmanuel Jal— Warchild." *The Guardian* (May 9, 2008): 14.

Derrida, Jacques. *Dissemination.* Trans. Barbara Johnson. Chicago: University of Chicago Press, 1981.

Didcock, Barry. "A Chance for Peace." *Sunday Herald* (July 16, 2006).

Diop, Boubacar Boris. *Murambi: The Book of Bones.* Bloomington: Indiana University Press, 2006.

Diouf, Mamadou. "Afterword." In *Makers and Breakers: Children and Youth in Postcolonial Africa,* ed. Alcinda Honwana and Filip de Boeck. Oxford: James Currey, Africa World Press & Codesria, 2005: pages 229–234.

———. "Engaging Postcolonial Cultures: African Youth and Public Space."
    African Studies Review 46.1 (September 2003): 1–12.

Dongala, Emmanuel. *Johnny Mad Dog.* Trans. Maria Louise Ascher. New
    York: Picador / Farrar, Straus, Giroux, 2005.

———. *An Introduction to Nigerian Government and Politics.* Bloomington:
    Indiana University Press, 1982.

Duin, Julia. "Ugandan to Testify to Civil War Horrors; Hill Panel to Hear of
    Sex Slavery." *Washington Times* (April 26, 2006): 6.

Dunson, Donald. *Child, Victim, Soldier: The Loss of Innocence in Uganda.*
    Maryknoll, NY: Orbis Books, 2008.

Emecheta, Buchi. *Destination Biafra.* Oxford: Heinemann, 1982.

"Eritrea-Ethiopia: End to Use of Child Soldiers Urged." www.irinnews.org.
    July 11, 2000.

"Eritrean Child Soldier Memoir Contains Errors, Publisher Admits."
    Agence France-Presse (April 18, 2008).

Farah, Nuruddin. *Links.* New York: Riverhead Books, 2004.

Fine, Sean, and Andrea Nix Fine. *War Dance.* THINKFilm, 2007.

Foster, Sarah. "Now I Know How It Feels to Cry." *Northern Echo* (May 27,
    2004): 12.

Gare, Shelley. "Africa's War Child." *Weekend Australian* (January 19, 2008):
    15.

Gettleman, Jeffrey. "Armed and Underage." *New York Times Upfront*
    (October 4, 2010). upfrontmagazine.com.

Goldberg, Elizabeth, and Alexandra Schultheis Moore, eds. *Theoretical
    Perspectives on Human Rights and Literature.* New York: Routledge,
    2012.

Harrow, Kenneth W. "The *Amalek* Factor: Child Soldiers and the
    Impossibility of Representation." *Postcolonial Text* 8.2 (2013): 1–20.

Holden, Philip. "Other Modernities: National Autobiography and
    Globalization." *Biography* 28.1 (Winter 2005): 89–103.

Honwana, Alcinda. *Child Soldiers in Africa.* Philadelphia: University of
    Pennsylvania Press, 2006.

Honwana, Alcinda, and Filip de Boeck. "Introduction: Children and
    Youth in Africa, Agency, Identity and Place." In *Makers and Breakers:
    Children and Youth in Postcolonial Africa,* ed. Alcinda Honwana and
    Filip de Boeck. Oxford: James Currey, Africa World Press & Codesria,
    2005: pages 1–18.

Hove, Chenjerai. *Bones.* Oxford: Heinemann, 1988.

Hovil, Lucy, and Zachary Lomo. "Whose Justice? Perceptions of Uganda's
    Amnesty Act 2000: The Potential for Conflict Resolution and
    Long-Term Reconciliation." Refugee Law Project Working Paper 15
    (February 2005). refugeelawproject.org.

Hungerford, Amy. "Memorizing Memory." *Yale Journal of Criticism* 14.1
    (Spring 2001): 67–92.

"Ishmael Beah." www.ishmaelbeah.com.

Iweala, Uzodinma. *Beasts of No Nation.* New York: Harper Perennial, 2005.

Jal, Emmanuel. *Warchild.* Sonic, 2008.

Jal, Emmanuel, with Megan Lloyd Davies. *War Child: A Child Soldier's
    Story.* New York: St. Martin's Press, 2009.

Jarrett-Macauley, Delia. *Moses, Citizen, and Me.* London: Granta, 2005.

"Johnny Mad Dog." *Kirkus Reviews* 73.6 (March 15, 2005).

"Judy A. Bernstein." https://www.goodreads.com/author/show/83160.
    Judy_A_Bernstein. September 24, 2017.

Kabir, Ananya Jahanara. "Affect, Body, Place: Trauma Theory in the
    World." In *The Future of Trauma Theory,* ed. Gert Buelens, Sam
    Durrant, and Robert Eaglestone. London: Routledge / Taylor &
    Francis, 2014: pages 63–75.

Kamara, Mariatu, with Susan McClelland. *The Bite of the Mango.* Toronto:
    Annick Press, 2008.

Kameo, Elizabeth. "Keitetsi was Home-Breaker at 13—Govt." *The Monitor*
    (Uganda) (May 22, 2003).

Kearney, J. A. "The Representation of Child Soldiers in Contemporary
    African Fiction." *Journal of Literary Studies* 26.1 (March 2010): 67–94.

Keitetsi, China. *Child Soldier: Fighting for My Life.* London: Souvenir

Press, 2004.

———. Phone interview by Joya Uraizee. August 4, 2013.

Kourouma, Ahmadou. *Allah Is Not Obliged.* Trans. Frank Wynne. London: Vintage, 2007.

Krippner, Stanley, and Teresa M. McIntyre. "Overview: In the Wake of War." In *The Psychological Impact of War Trauma on Civilians: An International Perspective,* ed. Stanley Krippner and Teresa M. McIntyre. Westport, CT: Praeger, 2003: pages 1–14.

LaCapra, Dominick. *Writing History, Writing Trauma.* Baltimore: Johns Hopkins University Press, 2001.

Leiren-Young, Mark. "Director Kim Nguyen Gives a Voice to a Young War Witch in *Rebelle.*" *Georgia Straight* (October 17, 2012).

Lejeune, Philippe. *On Autobiography.* Trans. Katherine Leary. Minneapolis: University of Minnesota Press, 1989.

"The Lost Boys of Sudan." International Rescue Committee, 2018. www.rescue.org.

Malaba, Mbongeni. "The Legacy of Thomas Mofolo's 'Chaka.'" *English in Africa* 13.1 (May 1986): 61–71.

Malcolm, Janet. *The Journalist and the Murderer.* New York: Knopf, 1990.

Masemola, Kgomotso Michael. "Autobiography in Africa." In *The Novel in Africa and the Caribbean since 1950,* ed. Simon Gikandi. Vol. 11 of *The Oxford History of the Novel in English,* ed. Patrick Parrinder. Oxford: Oxford University Press, 2016: pages 344–358.

McClelland, Susan. "Books Will Motivate My People to Write [Interview with Mariatu Kamara]." *The Times* (London) (February 27, 2010).

McDonnell, Faith J. H., and Grace Akallo. *Girl Soldier: A Story of Hope for Northern Uganda's Children.* Grand Rapids, MI: Chosen Books, 2007.

McNally, Richard J. *Remembering Trauma.* Cambridge: Harvard University Press, 2003.

"Megan Lloyd Davies." www.meganlloyddavies.com.

Mehari, Senait. *Heart of Fire: One Girl's Extraordinary Journey from Child Soldier to Soul Singer.* Trans. Christine Lo. London: Profile Books,

2007.

Menchú, Rigoberta. *I, Rigoberta Menchú an Indian Woman in Guatemala.* Ed. Elisabeth Burgos-Debray. Trans. Ann Wright. New York: Verso, 2009.

Mengestu, Dinaw. "Children of War." *New Statesman* (June 18, 2007): 60–61.

Mengiste, Maaza. *Beneath the Lion's Gaze.* New York: Norton, 2010.

Millard, Rosie. "I'm Haunted by My Past as a Child Soldier." Interview with Senait Mehari. *Sunday Times* (London) (July 30, 2006).

Mofolo, Thomas. *Chaka the Zulu.* Trans. F. H. Dutton. Oxford: Oxford University Press, 1977.

Moore, Alexandra Schultheis, and Elizabeth Swanson Goldberg, eds. *Teaching Human Rights in Literary and Cultural Studies.* New York: MLA, 2015.

Moore, Jennifer. *Humanitarian Law in Action Within Africa.* New York: Oxford University Press, 2012.

Morrison, Jago. "Imagined Biafras: Fabricating Nation in Nigerian Civil War Writing." *ARIEL: A Review of International English Literature* 36.1–2 (January–April 2005): 5–25.

Musiyiwa, Ambrose. "'Something Beautiful and Strong': Interview with Delia Jarrett-Macauley, Winner of Orwell Prize for Political Writing." Blogcritics Books. November 4, 2006. blogcritics.org.

Nakazibwe, Carolyne. "Gov't Further Denies Child Soldier Documentary." *The Monitor* (Uganda) (May 16, 2003).

Nason, David, and Shelley Gare. "Beah's Flaws 'Poetic Licence.'" *The Australian* (January 21, 2008): 1, 6.

Neale, Timothy D. "'. . . the Credentials That Would Rescue Me': Trauma and the Fraudulent Survivor." *Holocaust and Genocide Studies* 24.3 (Winter 2010): 431–448.

Neill, Rosemary. "First Impressions." *Weekend Australian* (May 9, 2009).

Nelson, Diane M. "Indian Giver or Nobel Savage: Duping, Assumptions of Identity, and Other Double Entendres in Rigoberta Menchú Tum's

Stoll/en Past." *American Ethnologist* 28.2 (May 2001): 303–331.

Ngugi wa Thiong'o. *A Grain of Wheat.* London: Heinemann, 1967.

Nguyen, Kim. *War Witch (Rebelle).* Quebec: Mongrel Media, 2012.

"Nigeria; Mariatu's *The Bite of the Mango*." *Africa News* (May 15, 2009).

Nkashama, Pius Ngandu. "Les 'enfants-soldats' et les guerres coloniales: À travers le premier roman africain." *Études littéraires* 35.1 (2003): 29–40.

Nwapa, Flora. *Never Again.* Enugu, Nigeria: Tana Press, 1975.

Okech, Joy. "Women Bear the Brunt of LRA Insurgents." NewsfromAFRICA, July 2004. newsfromafrica.org.

Pederson, Joshua. "Speak, Trauma: Toward a Revised Understanding of Literary Trauma Theory." *Narrative* 22.3 (October 2014): 333–353.

Piers, Craig C. "Remembering Trauma: A Characterological Perspective." In *Trauma and Memory,* ed. Linda M. Williams and Victoria L. Banyard. Thousand Oaks, CA: Sage, 1999: pages 57–65.

Pratt, Mary Louise. "*I, Rigoberta Menchú* and the 'Culture Wars.'" In *The Rigoberta Menchú Controversy,* ed. Arturo Arias. Minneapolis: University of Minnesota Press, 2001: pages 29–48.

Provencher, Raymonde, dir. *Faith, Grace, Lucy, Child Soldiers.* National Film Board of Canada, 2010.

"Questions and Answers on the Recruitment and Use of Child Soldiers." United Nations Office of the Special Representative of the Secretary-General for Children and Armed Conflict. February 12, 2016.

Romero, Frances. "A Sudanese Lost Boy, Found." *Time* (February 5, 2009). content.time.com.

Sachs, Andrea. "Galley Girl Catches Up with Uzodinma Iweala." *Time* (November 29, 2005). content.time.com.

Sanders, Mark. "Culpability and Guilt: Child Soldiers in Fiction and Memoir." *Law and Literature* 23.2 (Summer 2011): 195–223.

Saro-Wiwa, Ken. *Sozaboy: A Novel in Rotten English.* New York: Pearson/Longman, 2010.

Sawyer, Kem Knapp. *Out in Front: Grace Akallo and the Pursuit of Justice for Child Soldiers.* Greensboro, NC: Morgan Reynolds, 2015.

Schaffer, Kay, and Sidonie Smith. *Human Rights and Narrated Lives: The Ethics of Recognition.* New York: Palgrave Macmillan, 2004.

Schultheis, Alexandra W. "Global Specters: Child Soldiers in the Postnational Fiction of Uzodinma Iweala and Chris Abani." In *Emerging African Voices: A Study of Contemporary African Literature,* ed. Walter P. Collins III. New York: Cambria Press, 2010: pages 13–51.

Sen, Amartya. *Inequality Reexamined.* New York: Russell Sage Foundation and Harvard University Press, 1992.

Shaw, Rosalind. *Memories of the Slave Trade: Ritual and the Historical Imagination in Sierra Leone.* Chicago: University of Chicago Press, 2002.

Sides, Kirk B. "Relating to and through Land: An Ecology of Relations in Thomas Mofolo's *Chaka.*" In *The Postcolonial World,* ed. Jyotsna G. Singh and David D. Kim. New York: Routledge / Taylor & Francis, 2017: 439–457.

"Sierra Leone: Country Still Suffers Legacy of Child Soldiers." *Africa News* (April 25, 2012).

"Sierra Leone's Refugee All Stars." sierraleonesrefugeeallstars.com. July 30, 2018.

Slaughter, Joseph R. *Human Rights, Inc.: The World Novel, Narrative Form, and International Law.* New York: Fordham University Press, 2007.

Smith, Dinitia. "Young and Privileged, but Writing Vividly of Africa's Child Soldiers." *New York Times* (November 24, 2005): 1–2.

"Spotlight Turns on Africa's Lost Boys." *New Zealand Herald* (May 5, 2007). June 5, 2013.

Stephens, Sharon. "Introduction: Children and the Politics of Culture in 'Late Capitalism.'" In *Children and the Politics of Culture,* ed. Sharon Stephens. Princeton, NJ: Princeton University Press, 1995: pages 3–50.

Stoll, David. *Rigoberta Menchú and the Story of All Poor Guatemalans.* Boulder, CO: Westview Press, 1999.

Strehle, Susan. "Producing Exile: Diasporic Vision in Adichie's *Half of a Yellow Sun.*" *Modern Fiction Studies* (Baltimore) 57.4 (Winter 2011): 650–672.

Summerfield, Derek. "A Critique of Seven Assumptions behind Psychological Trauma Programmes in War-Affected Areas." *Social Science and Medicine* (Amsterdam) 48 (1999): 1449–1462.

———. "Cross Cultural Perspectives on the Medicalization of Human Suffering." In *Posttraumatic Stress Disorder: Issues and Controversies,* ed. Gerald M. Rosen. Hoboken, NJ: John Wiley, 2004: pages 233–245.

Swart, Genevieve. "Africa's Children Brought to Life, Brutally." *Sun Herald* (Sydney) (April 30, 2006).

Temmerman, Els de. *The Aboké Girls: Children Abducted in Northern Uganda.* Kampala, Uganda: Fountain Publishers, 2000.

"Thousands of Slaves in Sudan." *BBC News, Africa* (May 28, 2003). http://news.bbc.co.uk/2/hi/africa/2942964.stm.

UNICEF. "The Paris Principles. Principles and Guidelines on Children Associated with Armed Forces or Armed Groups." February 2007. www.unhcr.org.

Uwakweh, Pauline. "(Re)Constructing Masculinity and Femininity in African War Narratives: The Youth in Chimamanda Adichie's *Half of a Yellow Sun* and Gorretti Kyomuhendo's *Waiting: A Novel of Uganda at War.*" *JALA: Journal of the African Literature Association* 7.1 (June 2012): 82–106.

Valdes, Marcela. "A Long Look Home." *Publishers Weekly* 252.24 (June 13, 2005): 26–28.

van der Kok, Bessel A., and Onno van der Hart. "The Intrusive Past: The Flexibility of Memory and the Engraving of Trauma." *American Imago* (Baltimore) 48.4 (1991): 425–454.

Vassilatos, Alexia. "The Transculturation of Thomas Mofolo's *Chaka.*" *Tydskrif Vir Letterkunde* 53.2 (2016): 161–174.

"Verlagsgruppe Droemer Knaur." www.holtzbrinck.com.

Walford, Lynn. "Truth, Lies and Politics in the Debate over Testimonial

Writing: The Cases of Rigoberta Menchú and Binjamin Wilkomirski."
The Comparatist (North Carolina) 30 (May 2006): 113–121.

Wasike, Alfred. "Gov't Launches Documentary to Counter China Keitetsi
Abuse Claim." *New Vision* (Uganda) (May 22, 2003).

Watters, Ethan. *Crazy Like Us: The Globalization of the American Psyche.*
New York: Free Press, 2010.

Whitehead, Anne. "Representing the Child Soldier: Trauma,
Postcolonialism and Ethics in Delia Jarrett-Macauley's *Moses, Citizen
and Me.*" In *Ethics and Trauma in Contemporary British Fiction,* ed.
Susana Onega and Jean-Michel Ganteau. Amsterdam: Rodopi, 2011:
pages 241–263.

"Who We Are." Institute on Religion and Democracy. www.theird.org.

"Women and Gender; If African Women Do Not Tell Their Own Narratives
No One Else Will." *The Nation* (Nairobi) (December 12, 2010).

Wood, Liana. "Young Mr. Death." *New Statesman* (London), April 6, 2009:
53.

Index

(nn.2–3); National Resistance
Army (NRA) of, 27–28, 29;
religion in, 52
Uwakweh, Pauline, 97

Walford, Lynn, 106 (n.8)
War Child (film), 36, 68
Watters, Ethan, 15

Wessells, Michael, 18
Whitehead, Anne, 19, 92
Wilkomirski, Binjamin, 20–21, 106 (n.8)
Williams, Kabba, 44, 107 (n.2)

Yohannes, Almaz, 35